The Intrepid Leader

How to Triumph Where Others Fear

Courage, Character, and the Code of Modern Leadership

by

Robert N. Jacobs
MSc

All rights reserved
Copyright © Robert N. Jacobs, 2025
The right of Robert N. Jacobs to be identified as the author of this work has been asserted in accordance with Section 78 of the Copyright, Designs and Patents Act 1988
The book cover is copyright to Robert N. Jacobs
This book is published by
Growth Seeker Publishing Ltd.

Growth Seeker Publishing

This book is sold subject to the conditions that it shall not, by way of trade or otherwise, be lent, resold, hired out or otherwise circulated without the author's or publisher's prior consent in any form of binding or cover other than that in which it is published and without a similar condition including this condition being imposed on the subsequent purchaser.
This book is a work of fiction. Any resemblance to people or events, past or present, is purely coincidental.
ISBN: 9798319438355

"Intrepid leadership is not about grand speeches or chasing applause; it's the fearless commitment to taking decisive action where others hesitate. It's about having the courage to confront uncertainty head-on, rooted in an unwavering character that refuses to compromise on integrity, even under immense pressure. Intrepid leaders are grounded in self-discipline and unshakeable faith in a guiding mission that transcends personal ambition. They turn challenges into stepping stones, setbacks into growth opportunities, and trials into tests of resilience and character.

Great leadership, then, isn't defined by a position of power or an impressive title. It's measured by your capacity to serve, inspire, and elevate those around you through clarity of vision, genuine empathy, and the relentless pursuit of meaningful results. Great leadership is the consistent demonstration of honour, humility, and adaptability. It is not about seeking control; it is about cultivating trust and respect through authentic service and ethical influence. Great leaders create not just followers but a legacy, inspiring others to become courageous leaders themselves."

Robert N. Jacobs

"Your greatest victory begins when you master yourself first, stand by your principles even when it's hard, and lift others through every storm with unwavering honour."

Robert N. Jacobs

Foreword

You are about to enter a realm where leadership steps beyond stale theory and buzzwords. You might have wondered if you truly have what it takes to guide others, especially when the stakes are high. In these pages, you will discover that you do. You will see how courage is not reserved for a chosen few and how character can shine through any challenge you face. You will realise that genuine leadership is neither for the loudest nor the flashiest but for those bold enough to act on their convictions when others hesitate.

Unlike other leadership books you have skimmed or seen stacked on shelves, this one will not drown you in complicated models or endless anecdotes about grand CEOs. Instead, it cuts to the heart of what transforms a person from a bystander into a force for good. You will find lessons drawn from real experiences, from the quiet moments that test your values to the high-pressure decisions that can redefine your future. You will learn how to craft your own code of modern leadership, one that is anchored in unwavering principles but ready to adapt to today's lightning-fast world.

Every chapter is designed to show you new ways to think, to sharpen your focus, and to move you to take action. As you turn these pages, you will see that fear is not your enemy, inaction is. You will recognise how a disciplined life opens doors you never knew existed and how empathy is the secret ingredient that can rally others around a shared mission. More than that, you will walk away with a sense of confidence that stands firm, even when nothing else does.

Leadership is not an abstract idea. It is a daily practice that affects everything, from the targets you set at work to the example you set for your family to how you carry yourself in your community. This book does not sugarcoat the trials you will face. Instead, it arms you with the courage and clarity to face them head-on. You will uncover tools, mindsets, and battle-tested principles that ensure you remain steady in a chaotic world.

You are invited now to step onto the path of the intrepid leader. You will not be told to follow one rigid formula. You will be guided to develop a style that is authentically yours, one that honours your values and still manages to break new ground. My hope is that you will treat each insight as a personal challenge: something to test, refine, and finally make your own.

Take a deep breath. Look ahead to the road that will test your resolve, call forth your strengths, and shape the best version of you. Once you set foot on it, you will see why real leadership does not wait for permission. It starts the moment you decide to act. So, stand tall, blaze ahead, and never forget that the potential to lead with honour and bravery already lives within you.

Table of Contents

CHAPTER 1

Leading Yourself First: The Mastery Of Self-Leadership .. 1

1. The 'Leader of One' Philosophy 2

2. Building Self-Discipline: The Power of Daily Habits 4

3. Emotional Control: Mastering Your Mind Under Pressure 7

4. Character Over Charisma: Why Integrity Matters More 9

5. The Role of Faith and Conviction in Leadership 11

Conclusion 14

CHAPTER 2

The Leadership Mindset: Thinking Like A Great Leader.. 16

1. The Difference Between Bosses and Leaders 17

2. The Paradox of Power: Strength Through Humility 19

3. The Growth Mindset: How Leaders Stay Adaptable 21

4. Building Resilience: Handling Failure Like a Warrior ... 23

5. Vision vs. Execution: Seeing the Big Picture While Taking Small Steps 26

Conclusion 28

CHAPTER 3

The Art Of Influence: How To Earn Respect And Trust 30

1. Why Leadership is About Service, Not Control 30

2. The Law of Reciprocity: Give Before You Expect 33

3. The Power of Listening: How to Lead Without Speaking 35

 4. Building an Unshakable Reputation Through Consistency 38

 5. The Science of Persuasion: How to Move People Without Forcing Them 40

 Conclusion 43

CHAPTER 4

Leadership In Action: Decision-Making Under Pressure 45

 1. The 70% Rule: Why Perfect Decisions Don't Exist 45

 2. Courage Over Comfort: Making Hard Choices 48

 3. The Role of Instinct vs. Data in Leadership 50

 4. Risk-Taking: When to Be Bold, When to Be Cautious .. 53

 5. Course Correction: Admitting When You're Wrong 55

 Conclusion 58

CHAPTER 5

The Warrior's Path: Strength, Honour, And Grit 60

 1. Why Every Great Leader Faces Trials and Hardships .. 61

 2. Mental Toughness: How to Stay Strong in Chaos 63

 3. The Code of Honour: Leading with Integrity 66

 4. Strength with Compassion: Balancing Power and Kindness 68

 5. Fighting the Inner Enemy: Overcoming Doubt, Fear, and Ego 71

 Conclusion 74

CHAPTER 6

Leading In The Digital Age: Influence In A Changing World 76

 1. The Social Media Trap: Leadership Beyond Likes and Follows 77

2. Building Real Influence in a World of Short Attention Spans 79

3. The Digital Revolution: How AI, Tech, and Automation Impact Leadership 81

4. Crisis Management in a Hyperconnected World 84

5. The Return to Authenticity: Why Old-School Leadership Still Wins 87

Conclusion 89

CHAPTER 7

Leading Through Crisis: What To Do When Everything Falls Apart 92

1. The Calm in the Storm: How Great Leaders Handle Crisis 93

2. The Psychology of Panic: Leading Others When Fear Takes Over 95

3. Decision-Making in Chaos: Separating Noise from What Matters 98

4. The Power of Ownership: Taking Responsibility for Failures 100

5. How to Rebuild Trust After a Leadership Mistake 103

Conclusion 105

CHAPTER 8

The Legacy Of A Leader: Mentorship And Impact 107

1. Why Great Leaders Don't Create Followers, They Create More Leaders 107

2. The Power of Mentorship: Investing in the Next Generation 110

3. Servant Leadership: Putting Others Before Yourself . 113

4. How to Leave a Legacy That Outlives You 115

5. The Final Test of Leadership: Stepping Away with Honour 118

Conclusion 121

CHAPTER 9

The Leadership Paradoxes: The Hidden Secrets Of Great Leaders 123

1. Lead by Following: The Wisdom of Lifelong Learning 124

2. Strength Through Vulnerability: Why Admitting Mistakes Builds Trust 126

3. More Discipline, More Freedom: How Structure Creates Success 128

4. Control vs. Trust: Knowing When to Let Go 131

5. Leading Without a Title: Influence Beyond Position ...134

Conclusion 137

CHAPTER 10

The Leadership Code: Your Personal Blueprint For Success 138

1. Creating Your Own Leadership Philosophy 139

2. Developing a Personal Code of Honour 141

3. How to Stay True to Your Values Under Pressure 143

4. The Daily Rituals of Great Leaders 146

5. The Final Step: Walking the Path of Leadership Every Day 149

Conclusion 152

CHAPTER 1

Leading Yourself First: The Mastery Of Self-Leadership

You stand on the edge of a new chapter in your life. You might question whether you have the grit, the discipline, or the inner fire to step into a leadership role. There is a voice inside you that whispers doubts: it reminds you of every flaw and every time you fell short. Yet deep within, there is another voice urging you forward. It challenges you to become the kind of person who directs your own path before guiding others. Leadership of any magnitude begins with the one individual you can fully control: yourself.

In the modern world, leadership is often mistaken for titles, flashy presentations, or social media profiles filled with empty promises. That is not real leadership. True leadership is an intimate journey that starts in your own mind. It takes shape in your habits, your standards, and the way you handle your emotions. It reveals itself in the reflection you see in the mirror every morning. The greatest leaders in history, from commanders on ancient battlefields to innovators who disrupted entire industries, share one common trait. They have all excelled at leading themselves before they guided armies or influenced markets.

You will explore the core ingredients of self-leadership in this chapter. You will discover the power in disciplining yourself long before you demand discipline from anyone else. You will see how mastering your emotions under pressure can be the difference between success and failure. You will learn that integrity holds greater weight than any flashy charm. You will also delve into the influence of faith and unwavering conviction in shaping your approach to leadership. This is your invitation to step onto that road and walk forward with strength, poise, and authenticity. Prepare to build the foundation upon which all genuine leadership stands.

1. The 'Leader of One' Philosophy

You might imagine leaders as those who command vast organisations or rally armies to victory. Yet, before you control large teams or inspire entire communities, you must first be the ruler of your own world. The essence of the 'Leader of One' philosophy revolves around taking full responsibility for your actions, your decisions, and your development. When you prove to yourself that you can stay disciplined and hold yourself accountable, you establish the credibility needed to guide others down that same road.

Winston Churchill once remarked that the price of greatness is responsibility. When he took on the role of Prime Minister during World War II, he did not merely direct strategies or hold rousing press conferences. He also forced himself to live by the demands he placed on others. He ate modestly during rationing, worked long hours in bomb shelters, and stayed unwavering in the midst of crisis. He was, in effect, the first soldier in the battle he asked his nation to fight. That unflinching sense of personal accountability lay at the core of his leadership.

In your life, the 'Leader of One' philosophy demands a similar level of personal discipline. You might have ambitions of launching a startup, serving your community, or transforming your family's future. Great. But you must begin by setting the standards you want others to follow. If you wish to see punctuality on your team, be the first to arrive at meetings. If you expect excellence in output, ensure your own work is polished to the highest level. If you want to encourage moral behaviour in society, make sure your private conduct mirrors that principle.

Recent research from the Harvard Business Review suggests that teams led by individuals who practise self-discipline display higher engagement and lower turnover. That is because people sense authenticity. They see when a leader lives by the same rules that he or she proclaims. When you embody the principles you preach, you become a beacon of credibility. Credibility fosters trust, and trust is the cornerstone of any successful group effort.

Mastering the 'Leader of One' philosophy also involves self-awareness. You cannot lead yourself effectively if you remain ignorant of your own blind spots. You need to assess your strengths, shortcomings, and triggers. Ask yourself what situations test your patience or prompt you to cut corners. By spotting these internal pitfalls, you can lay down strategies to keep them from derailing your journey. Reflection might involve journaling, seeking genuine feedback from those around you, or simply examining your past reactions to pressure. When you become transparent with yourself, you create room to grow and evolve.

Another key pillar of this philosophy is guarding your mindset. External challenges will arise, but the strongest battles are fought within. If your internal chatter is defeatist, you risk sabotaging your own potential. If you keep a strong, focused outlook, you equip yourself to handle setbacks with composure and tenacity. That requires conscious effort. Many who practise the 'Leader of One' philosophy use affirmations, mindfulness techniques, or quiet moments of reflection to steady their mental compass. These strategies are not merely modern trends. They are proven tools for optimising your internal environment so that it aligns with your mission.

You might wonder if self-leadership means striving for perfection. Absolutely not. It means pursuing progress and aiming to be a better version of yourself each day. Perfection is a mirage. It is unattainable and often leads to frustration. Embrace the reality that you will make mistakes. Acknowledge them, learn from them, and adapt your approach. Self-leadership is as much about growth as it is about responsibility.

When you genuinely adopt the 'Leader of One' philosophy, you create a robust base upon which every other leadership principle rests. You become not just a person who issues directives, but a person who lives out the standards you champion. That authenticity sets you apart in a world where far too many leaders say one thing and do another. By ruling over your own inner world, you show others the unshakeable foundation that true leadership stands upon.

2. Building Self-Discipline: The Power of Daily Habits

You hold grand aspirations. You want to steer teams with clarity, bring fresh vision to stagnant workplaces, or uplift entire communities. None of that will be possible without self-discipline. This quality is neither glamorous nor instantly rewarding. Yet it is the silent force that enables you to remain steadfast when your peers lose focus, your circumstances become hostile, and your energy levels waver.

Former Navy SEAL commander Jocko Willink, well-known for his approach to daily routine, emphasises the critical role of habits in shaping a disciplined life. He preaches an early wake-up call coupled with rigorous exercise, not merely to post motivational pictures but to master his own mind every dawn. By practising self-discipline first thing in the morning, you essentially tell yourself that you are in control of your agenda. You do not bow to the comfort of a warm bed or the lure of putting tasks off for later. You cement your authority over your actions before distractions can creep in.

In your quest for leadership, daily habits are your greatest allies. Commit to small, consistent actions that align with the traits you wish to see in yourself. Perhaps you decide to read ten pages of a leadership book each day. You might commit to finishing each workday with fifteen minutes of reflection, noting one success and one lesson learned. Another habit might involve setting aside a short period in the afternoon for deep focus, where you work without social media or unnecessary interruptions. The specifics matter less than the consistency. Repetition of small behaviours leads to large-scale transformation.

Scientific studies have backed the idea that habit formation relies on both repetition and motivation. A study by University College London found that it takes an average of 66 days to solidify a new habit. That initial period demands willpower. You might feel excited on day one, confident on day two, and then exhausted or distracted by day seven. This is where your commitment to discipline is tested. Keep going. Push through any urge to quit or postpone. Once you pass the threshold where your new behaviour becomes second nature, you release valuable mental energy for more demanding tasks.

Self-discipline also hinges on balancing routine with adaptability. You should not lock yourself into a rigid schedule that collapses the moment life happens. Instead, identify the non-negotiables in your day and make sure those remain intact even if you have to shuffle timings. If your daily workout does not happen at dawn because of a shift in your work schedule, reschedule it for the afternoon or evening. Discipline is not about robotic perfection. It is about refusing to make excuses and sticking to your priorities under changing circumstances.

Be selective with the habits you adopt. Some individuals try to overhaul every aspect of their life overnight, leading to burnout and eventual relapse. Focus on key areas that fuel your leadership journey. That might be physical fitness for mental clarity, dedicated reading time for continued learning, or strict boundaries on your phone usage to free up creative space. Start with a few targeted changes, execute them consistently, and watch how those small investments multiply your capacity over time.

The beauty of daily habits is that they act like a silent trainer, shaping your identity day after day. When you repeat the same disciplined action, you reaffirm to yourself who you are. You become the type of person who does not skip workouts, who finishes tasks on schedule, or who invests in personal development. Your actions no longer hinge on fleeting moods or external pressures. They follow your chosen standards. You free yourself from the tyranny of momentary impulses.

Finally, never forget that self-discipline is not an act of punishment. It is a gift you give yourself to unlock your highest potential. When you see discipline as a form of self-respect, you transform your daily habits into powerful statements of purpose. You do not rely on bursts of motivation to keep you moving forward. You rely on your unwavering routines. You prove to yourself that you can direct your life with intent, and that is a hallmark of a leader who commands respect and admiration.

3. Emotional Control: Mastering Your Mind Under Pressure

You will face moments that push your emotional limits. The sting of betrayal, the stress of meeting impossible deadlines, the frustration of dealing with difficult personalities. These situations test the depth of your leadership. If you do not hold the reins of your emotional world, your ability to make clear decisions and maintain trust in those around you will vanish. Emotional control is not about pretending that you have no feelings. It is about acknowledging those feelings, understanding their impact, and choosing responses that serve the bigger purpose.

British F1 driver Lewis Hamilton offers a strong example of mastering emotions under severe pressure. During tight championship battles, Hamilton keeps a cool demeanour inside a cockpit that is heating to over 50 degrees Celsius. He remains focused on precise data while adrenaline threatens to spike. He has spoken publicly about using breathing exercises and mental imagery to stay composed in tense situations. That discipline has helped him secure multiple world titles and break records in a fiercely competitive sport.

Learning to direct your emotional responses begins with self-awareness. When you understand your triggers, you can intercept knee-jerk reactions before they spiral out of control. Do you notice a spike of anger when faced with abrupt changes in plans. Do you shut down when you sense criticism. Take note of these internal cues. In the beginning, you might only see them in hindsight. That is fine. Each time you reflect on a moment where your emotions got the better of you, you gain valuable lessons on how to respond differently next time.

Leading Yourself First: The Mastery Of Self-Leadership

Training your mind to remain calm under fire can involve physical and mental strategies. Breathing techniques are one proven method. A simple approach is to inhale for four counts, hold for four counts, then exhale for four counts. This lowers your heart rate and keeps you grounded in the present. You can also use immediate re-framing techniques. Instead of dwelling on how a setback reflects on your competence, ask yourself what opportunity might arise from it. Instead of lashing out at an unhelpful teammate, ask how you can address the root cause of the conflict.

Some leaders utilise short mental breaks when they feel emotions boiling. Stepping away from a heated conversation or taking a brief walk can reset your mindset. This is not running away. It is preventing a moment of tension from escalating into a full-blown crisis. Emotional control can save relationships, maintain team cohesion, and preserve your capacity to think strategically when it counts. A calm mind is a powerful mind.

Research from the American Psychological Association points out that individuals who regularly practise emotional regulation techniques experience reduced stress levels and enhanced problem-solving abilities. This is not just motivational talk. It is a scientifically supported truth. The better you manage your emotional volatility, the more mental resources you have for tackling complex challenges.

In leading yourself, emotional control sets the tone for your environment. If you react with outrage or panic, you give others tacit permission to lose their composure as well. On the other hand, if you stay balanced and objective, you create an atmosphere where rational discussion prevails. People look to you for emotional cues. When you set a standard of poise, you empower your group to navigate high-pressure scenarios without descending into chaos.

Ultimately, emotional control is about fortifying your resilience. It is about rising above temporary frustrations to see the long game. You will have to address strong emotions. That is part of being human. The difference is that you will not let those emotions steer the ship. You will be at the helm, making choices guided by your principles and long-term objectives. This quality, harnessed through practice and self-awareness, separates those who collapse under strain from those who rise to every challenge with unshakeable composure.

4. Character Over Charisma: Why Integrity Matters More

You will meet individuals who shine brightly on social media or in boardrooms with their charm. They captivate crowds with witty lines, sparkling banter, or memorable taglines. Yet, when challenges strike, their facade of confidence can crack if it is not anchored by strong character. Charisma can draw people in, but it is integrity that keeps people loyal. Your followers, colleagues, or community will quickly see if your external persona does not align with your true self. That gap will cause doubt and erode trust. Charisma might excite people for a while, but a solid character is what sustains genuine influence.

One real-life illustration comes from Alan Mulally, who served as the CEO of Ford Motor Company starting in 2006. He took over at a time when the company was veering toward financial disaster. Mulally was not a leader who dazzled his audience with grandiose speeches. Instead, he showed humility, transparency, and a firm moral compass. He openly shared the state of the company's troubles, took accountability for difficult decisions, and asked his top executives to do the same. While his manner was approachable, it was his reliability and ethical standards that ultimately led Ford back to profitability without a government bailout. His tenure stands as proof that people will follow a trustworthy leader even through painful restructuring. He built confidence through straight talk and responsible actions.

When you put character first, you make choices guided by moral principles, even when it would be easier to take shortcuts. This demands honesty, accountability, and moral courage. Your true test will arrive in moments where no one else is watching. Will you keep your commitments. Will you own up to mistakes instead of shifting the blame. Will you maintain the highest standards when a lesser path seems more profitable or popular. The answers to these questions define the strength of your character.

Integrity also plays a crucial part in building genuine relationships. You may create instant rapport with wit, but deeper bonds form when individuals trust that your word is your bond. They need to see that you do not manipulate situations to your advantage or tolerate misconduct within your team. If you ever slip, and everyone does at some point, character demands that you address the situation and make it right. That level of accountability fosters a culture of honesty where people are not scared to speak up about problems or highlight flaws in the system.

Research conducted by the Ethics & Compliance Initiative shows that organisations led by individuals who emphasise integrity have lower incidents of fraud, improved workforce morale, and stronger financial performance. The alignment between ethical leadership and sustainable results is not accidental. Integrity eliminates the costly distractions that come from legal troubles, internal conflicts, or plummeting public image.

If you rely solely on charm, you run the risk of building relationships on fragile foundations. Over time, people will notice inconsistencies in your words and actions. A single scandal or moment of dishonesty can undo years of glitzy brand-building. The resulting fallout can be devastating, both for your leadership journey and for anyone who depends on your guidance. Charm might make you an enticing figure in the short run, but it is no substitute for moral fortitude.

Choose integrity at every crossroads. Uphold your values even when it hurts your immediate interests. Defend them when others pressure you to compromise. By doing so, you establish an unshakable reputation that can weather storms. This is the kind of grounded leadership that people remember, respect, and willingly follow. It also gives you peace of mind, knowing that you are acting in alignment with your highest principles. Remember that leadership, at its core, is not about being the most magnetic person in the room. It is about guiding others toward what is right, fair, and honourable. If you stand firm in character, you will find that your influence reaches far beyond momentary applause or fleeting trends.

5. The Role of Faith and Conviction in Leadership

You cannot become a strong leader by clinging to uncertain beliefs or half-hearted goals. When your convictions are shallow, you will buckle at the first sign of resistance. True leadership requires faith in something greater than yourself, whether that is faith in a spiritual sense or faith in a core mission. This type of conviction does more than simply guide your actions. It acts as an anchor that holds you steady when external forces threaten to topple you.

An example of unwavering faith shaping leadership is that of Harriet Tubman. Although best known for leading enslaved individuals to freedom through the Underground Railroad, Tubman also served as a nurse and a spy during the American Civil War. She credited her unyielding resolve to a deep spiritual belief that she was fulfilling a higher purpose. That faith gave her the courage to venture into dangerous territories, rescue people under extreme risk, and do it repeatedly without hesitation. She did not have corporate resources or political influence at her disposal. Her power came from a fervent belief that her actions served a moral imperative.

In your own life, faith can mean different things. For some, it is grounded in religious practices or a relationship with God. For others, it might be a dedication to a moral principle like justice, compassion, or patriotism. Some leaders find their faith in the mission of scientific progress or humanitarian service. The important element is having a guiding force that does not waver with everyday stress. You hold onto it when you are faced with costly decisions. It gives you the moral and emotional reserves to move forward with confidence.

Conviction is the outward expression of that faith. It shows up in the way you speak about your goals, the risks you choose to take, and the passion you bring to solving complex problems. Followers will sense that your drive goes beyond personal ambition. They see that you are propelled by something deeper than short-term gains. That level of commitment fosters loyalty. When you face adversity, you can point to that central belief as your reason to keep fighting.

Modern leadership expert Simon Sinek has highlighted the importance of starting with a "why." While many leaders focus on what they do or how they do it, the most influential leaders communicate why they are passionate about their mission. This resonates with people's emotions, fuelling trust and shared purpose. If you do not have a solid conviction, you will struggle to convey a compelling reason for others to follow you. You might present polished slides or articulate grand plans, but without genuine belief, your words ring hollow.

Faith and conviction also act as your moral compass when dilemmas arise. They guide you to uphold your core values when external pressures tempt you to compromise. Whether you are weighing a financially profitable but ethically questionable move or deciding whether to speak up against injustice in your sphere of influence, your convictions will provide clarity. Without that anchor, you might find yourself drifting, chasing fleeting rewards or approval.

Be mindful that faith and conviction should not close your ears to advice or evidence. Being dogmatic can lead to stubbornness and stagnation. Authentic faith empowers you to remain teachable because you know your deeper reason for being. You can adjust tactics, learn from constructive criticism, and even revise certain methods, all while preserving the essence of what drives you. That is how lasting leadership takes form.

Ultimately, you must be willing to stake your reputation, your comfort, and your time on what you believe. That readiness to stand firm when you could easily flee is a hallmark of conviction. People are drawn to leaders who hold an unshakeable certainty in their goals. Your faith does not have to mirror that of others, but it must be genuine and deeply rooted. If you have that unwavering anchor and the willingness to act upon it, you will set a standard that others feel compelled to meet. That force, more than any strategy or tool, can transform you into a leader who endures through chaos and emerges even stronger.

Conclusion

You have stepped into the realm of leadership at its most personal level. The lessons you have explored do not hinge on anyone else's cooperation or permission. They rely entirely on your willingness to master your own mind, habits, and moral compass. Leading yourself first is not a stepping stone. It is the very foundation upon which all your future leadership triumphs will rest.

Throughout this chapter, you examined the philosophy of being the 'Leader of One,' embracing the total ownership of your behaviours and decisions. You discovered the transformative power of self-discipline and how daily habits become the bedrock for long-term success. You also looked at the necessity of managing your emotions under pressure, recognising that composure in a crisis can make the difference between staying on course or drifting into chaos. You then turned your focus to integrity and learned that true leadership extends far beyond the spark of raw magnetism. Finally, you delved into the powerful roles that faith and conviction can play in grounding you during turbulent times.

Let these lessons sink in. Use them to shape your daily routines, your approach to challenges, and your relationships with others. Each principle lays the groundwork for more advanced leadership skills you will tackle in the coming chapters. The journey might feel solitary at times, but it is in this solitude that you forge the mental and moral strength to lead others with wisdom and authority.

Remember that leadership, at its core, is a choice you make every single day. It is the choice to step forward, to hold yourself to the highest standard, and to keep progressing when lesser minds would quit. You now have the initial blueprints to become the person you aspire to be. Cultivate your discipline, guard your integrity, control your emotions, and let your convictions fuel your pursuit. By leading yourself with unwavering resolve, you pave the way for genuine influence that can reshape the world around you. This is where you begin to transform doubts into certainty and vision into reality. Use your newfound foundation and step boldly into the next phase of your leadership development.

CHAPTER 2

The Leadership Mindset: Thinking Like A Great Leader

You have laid the groundwork for genuine leadership by first mastering yourself. Now, you are ready to step further into the mindset that separates those who merely command from those who truly inspire. If you want to thrive as a leader, you must sharpen the lens through which you view yourself, your mission, and the people under your guidance. Your mindset becomes your compass, guiding your approach to power, ambition, and even failure. When that compass points toward honour, humility, and growth, you unlock a style of leadership that stands resilient under any strain.

The chapters ahead will test your mental toughness. The modern world can be loud and distracting, making it easy to lose sight of essential leadership principles. You may feel pulled between personal ambition and the greater good, or you might wrestle with balancing bold risks against careful planning. In this chapter, you will explore how truly great leaders think. You will see how they draw strength from humility, how they adapt rapidly to change, and how they reframe failures as stepping stones toward victory. You will delve into the tough but necessary distinction between bosses and leaders, and you will discover why vision alone is never enough without the grit of execution. Prepare to refine the way you interpret challenges, expand your mental agility, and wield the kind of authority that invites others to follow willingly.

1. The Difference Between Bosses and Leaders

You have probably witnessed the classic "boss" figure at some point in your life. A boss issues directives, enforces rules, and sometimes clings to authority out of insecurity or pride. A leader, on the other hand, embodies responsibility and service. This is not a trivial distinction. It shapes your outlook on power, empathy, and the development of those who work alongside you. The difference lies in how you view your role and the people around you.

A boss often focuses on results alone, measuring success in metrics and spreadsheets. If you operate like a boss, you might push deadlines at the expense of morale or overlook the emotional dynamics that impact performance. A leader still cares about results but understands that real success emerges when you nurture both performance and people. You recognise that loyal, motivated individuals achieve stronger outcomes and remain committed through tough times.

Indra Nooyi, the former CEO of PepsiCo, demonstrated this mindset by paying close attention to her team's well-being. She once explained how she made it a point to write letters to employees' parents, expressing gratitude for their son's or daughter's contributions to the company. Her actions went beyond mere public relations. They showed a genuine care for employees as complete human beings, not just units of productivity. That approach fostered loyalty and propelled PepsiCo through significant global expansions and transformations.

In practical terms, if you want to operate as a leader rather than a boss, start by setting an example of personal accountability. Accept blame for errors on your watch and highlight the achievements of your team. While a boss might react to errors with blame and anger, a leader views each mistake as a shared learning experience that can strengthen the entire group. This mindset builds trust. Your team will be honest about problems because they see you address them responsibly.

A boss might hoard information to maintain authority, whereas a leader seeks transparency. By sharing objectives, challenges, and even financial realities, you empower your team to offer meaningful solutions. If your people know the broader context, they are likelier to adapt creatively and stay united. You shed the illusion of authority by secrecy and prove that trust runs both ways.

Additionally, a boss might value compliance over independent thought, sometimes out of fear that strong-minded contributors could threaten control. A leader actively encourages open discussions, challenges to the status quo, and bold ideas. When you champion diverse perspectives, you expand the collective intelligence of your team. That readiness to invite dissenting voices might occasionally be uncomfortable, but it is vital for continuous improvement.

Research from Deloitte supports the idea that leaders who show empathy and inspire a shared vision tend to outperform those who rely on rigid commands. Their studies suggest that employees in such environments exhibit higher engagement and better problem-solving abilities. When people feel their contributions are valued, they invest more of their energy and creativity. That positive cycle elevates both output and workplace satisfaction.

Finally, the difference between bosses and leaders is seen in legacy. A boss might secure short-term gains through micromanagement or fear tactics, but those gains often unravel the moment they step away. A leader leaves behind a culture of self-motivation and ownership that persists long after they have moved on. Your ultimate objective as a leader is not only to hit targets but to empower others to grow, adapt, and eventually lead themselves. You become a catalyst who ignites a chain reaction of positive influence. That is the mark of genuine leadership.

2. The Paradox of Power: Strength Through Humility

It might seem counterintuitive that humility can amplify your authority, yet the greatest leaders through history understood this paradox well. It is easy to assume that power stems from status, wealth, or the ability to command. In reality, the most enduring influence often comes from an open and approachable style. When you show genuine humility, you invite others to speak candidly, to offer solutions you might not see, and to support you with sincere commitment rather than forced compliance.

Abraham Lincoln displayed this philosophy when he became President of the United States. He appointed rivals who had been his fiercest political opponents to his cabinet. His decision was not a sign of weakness. He wanted diverse viewpoints, even if those viewpoints clashed with his own. By giving those who challenged him a seat at the table, he harnessed a range of perspectives. That open-mindedness did not reduce his authority; it solidified it. People came to trust his decisions because he showed that he was not too proud to learn, to listen, and to refine his thinking.

In your own leadership journey, humility begins by acknowledging that you do not hold a monopoly on wisdom. You may have expertise in certain areas, but you are not faultless. When you own your gaps in knowledge, you encourage your team to step in and cover those gaps. If you walk around acting like an unassailable expert, you risk losing out on valuable insights. True confidence does not require you to pretend you have all the answers. It allows you to say, "I need your help" or "I was wrong" when it is warranted.

Humility also influences how you handle success. You will have moments where projects soar, goals are smashed, and your profile grows. A leader with humility credits the entire group and views victory as a collective achievement. This approach lifts morale and inspires loyalty. Conversely, an inflated ego that claims all the credit breeds resentment and quiet sabotage. Even if you achieved a milestone primarily through your own drive, you still rely on a network of people, resources, and circumstances. Recognising that fact keeps you grounded.

Recent studies from the Centre for Creative Leadership indicate that leaders who practise humble behaviours build stronger bonds and see improved team cohesion. Their research revealed that employees are more likely to share creative ideas and less likely to hide mistakes when they see a leader who does not dismiss input or punish vulnerability. When errors can be acknowledged early, you save time and resources by solving problems before they escalate.

Humility does not mean you allow yourself to be walked over. You can remain firm and decisive while still valuing the contributions of others. You can deliver criticism when necessary, but you do it in a way that shows you are genuinely interested in improvement rather than displaying dominance. You approach conflicts by seeking to understand the other person's viewpoint, which often defuses tension and paves the way for balanced solutions.

Another aspect of leading with humility is staying approachable. Create channels for open dialogue, whether that is one-on-one conversations, feedback surveys, or roundtable sessions. Make it known that you will not shoot down ideas prematurely or retaliate against those who disagree. This climate of respect attracts talented individuals who are eager to share expertise. Over time, you develop a culture where people are not just following orders but actively shaping the team's direction.

Ultimately, power without humility can foster arrogance, while humility without power can lead to timidity. The leader's job is to unite the two, projecting a steady confidence while welcoming the contributions of others. This paradox of power releases a strong current of loyalty, innovation, and resilience within your team. When you remain humble, you show a deep respect for the human element behind every success. That respect returns to you tenfold in the form of dedication, collaboration, and a willingness to endure difficult journeys by your side.

3. The Growth Mindset: How Leaders Stay Adaptable

You live in an era marked by rapid change, technological shifts, and unexpected disruptions. If you cling to a static mindset, you risk becoming obsolete before you realise what happened. The growth mindset, popularised by psychologist Carol Dweck, is more than a self-improvement slogan. It is a practical tool that sustains your capacity to adapt, learn, and innovate. At the core of this mindset is the belief that your talents and abilities are not fixed traits but can be developed through effort, strategy, and feedback.

When you embrace a growth mindset, you treat challenges as opportunities rather than threats. Imagine you are handed a complex project involving new technology you have never used. A fixed mindset might cause you to feel intimidated, perhaps even to shy away from accepting responsibility. With a growth mindset, you step up and say, "I can learn this. I may not be an expert yet, but I will figure it out." That confidence in the face of the unknown allows you to seize chances to grow, even if success is not guaranteed.

Many successful entrepreneurs credit their achievements to a willingness to pivot when the market shifts. Take Sara Blakely, the founder of Spanx. She had no prior background in fashion or business. Instead of letting that fact immobilise her, she immersed herself in learning about materials, sales tactics, and branding. She faced countless rejections, yet each "no" propelled her to refine her product and message. Her story highlights how adaptability can lead to breakthroughs that the status quo fails to see.

In practical terms, cultivating a growth mindset demands that you reframe failures. Instead of dwelling on them as permanent marks against your record, view them as feedback. This does not mean you ignore the cost of a mistake. You still need accountability. But rather than letting errors define you, you study them for lessons. Ask yourself what went wrong. Could you have anticipated the risk earlier. Did you undervalue a particular skill. Did you disregard somebody's advice too quickly. Extract the valuable lessons and move forward.

Research from Stanford University supports the link between a growth mindset and higher achievement across various domains, from education to corporate environments. Teams led by individuals who encourage flexible thinking and continuous improvement show greater agility in tackling new problems. They also tend to maintain higher morale because employees feel safe experimenting with new ideas. There is an undercurrent of shared curiosity that keeps everyone engaged.

One of the most direct ways to embed a growth mindset into your leadership style is to remain a lifelong student yourself. Maintain your learning through formal courses, online tutorials, or reading material outside your usual domain. If you want your team to keep evolving, you must demonstrate that no one ever stops growing. Attend workshops in areas where you feel less confident, and talk openly about the ways you are trying to improve. When your team observes that you are not locked in your own comfort zone, they will be more inclined to break out of theirs.

Be mindful of how you give feedback to others. Instead of praising them exclusively for natural ability, applaud their progress, problem-solving, or grit. This nurtures a culture where effort and learning are celebrated. People who receive such feedback are more likely to challenge themselves, try new approaches, and stay committed, even if they struggle at first. Your attention to how you frame both success and failure can shape the mindset of an entire organisation.

Staying adaptable does not require you to change your core values. Rather, it requires you to change your methods when circumstances evolve. If your values include excellence, integrity, and resilience, you can remain committed to those even if you pivot from one strategy to another. By marrying timeless principles with flexible thinking, you create a leadership approach that stands firm in purpose but fluid in execution. This combination helps you navigate uncertain waters and maintain the respect of those who count on you for guidance.

4. Building Resilience: Handling Failure Like a Warrior

Failure can break the spirit of those who are not prepared, but in your leadership journey, setbacks are inevitable. The question is not whether you will encounter defeat but how you will respond to it. If you develop resilience, you will face each new obstacle with a steadfast resolve, ready to learn, adapt, and push forward. True resilience is not about pretending you are unbreakable. It is about rising every time you are knocked down, wiser from the experience.

Angela Duckworth's research on grit provides a useful lens on resilience. In her studies, she noted that success correlates strongly with the ability to persevere in the face of adversity. Grit involves passion combined with consistent effort over the long run. It reminds you that natural brilliance or charm alone does not guarantee success. You need that warrior-like persistence to keep going when conditions turn harsh. Her work underscores the idea that you can develop greater tenacity with practice, much like you build muscle through regular exercise.

In building resilience, the first step is acknowledging the emotions that follow failure. If a project collapses or a significant partnership falls apart, you might feel disappointment, embarrassment, or even anger. Bottling up these feelings does not help. Instead, you can confront them directly and let them serve as proof that you care about the outcome. Next, channel that emotional energy into problem-solving. Refuse to let the setback define you. Ask yourself how you can rebuild momentum. Perhaps you can salvage certain elements of the project. Maybe you can pivot to a new approach. Reflect on what you have learned about your methods, your market, or even your internal blind spots.

Several high-profile figures have exemplified resilience by bouncing back from repeated failures. Colonel Harland Sanders faced countless rejections before his fried chicken concept took off and became a global franchise. Each rejection was an invitation to fine-tune his recipe, his pitch, and his determination. When he finally succeeded, people labelled him an overnight phenomenon, ignoring the relentless rejections that shaped his eventual triumph. His story highlights a core truth: Resilience is often an unglamorous stretch of repeated attempts until one approach finally sticks.

On a team level, resilience is built by fostering a culture that does not shame mistakes but studies them. If people fear harsh repercussions for every error, they will hide their missteps and avoid risk altogether. This results in a static environment where nobody ventures beyond safe boundaries. When you give your team the psychological safety to share errors openly, you can address them quickly and gather insights that benefit everyone. That openness accelerates learning and cuts down the time wasted in covering up mistakes.

Another aspect of resilience is physical and mental well-being. Chronic fatigue or unaddressed stress can erode your ability to cope with setbacks. Make it a priority to take care of your health. That includes proper sleep, nutrition, and stress management techniques such as mindfulness or breathing exercises. A worn-out leader struggles to remain resourceful in adversity. If you maintain your health, you keep your mind sharper and your attitude more balanced.

Finally, resilience is strengthened by having a support system. Great warriors do not fight alone. They rely on trusted allies. In your life, that might be a circle of mentors, peers, or advisers who can offer perspective or assist in picking up the pieces after a big failure. Surround yourself with people who bring positive energy and constructive criticism. Avoid the cynics who only see flaws and never propose solutions. When you enlist the help of strong supporters, you multiply your ability to recover. You draw upon their encouragement and insights to get back on your feet.

In the end, handling failure like a warrior means recognising that defeat is a natural component of growth. Each time you bounce back, you reaffirm your commitment to your mission and reinforce the mental toughness that sets leaders apart from followers. The journey will test your resilience again and again, but each setback presents a chance to sharpen your edge. Embrace that process, and you will emerge stronger, more capable, and far more inspiring to those who look to you for guidance.

5. Vision vs. Execution: Seeing the Big Picture While Taking Small Steps

Your ability to balance vision with execution can set you apart in a world overflowing with ideas but short on concrete accomplishments. A compelling vision galvanises people. It clarifies direction, fuels motivation, and keeps your team aligned on a shared purpose. Yet, vision without action is just wishful thinking. Execution transforms vision into tangible outcomes. The leader who excels in both realms becomes a force that drives long-term success.

Steve Jobs, co-founder of Apple, was known for his relentless focus on crafting products that captured the public imagination. He possessed a clear vision that centred on design excellence and user-friendly functionality. That vision alone, however, did not guarantee success. Jobs was also famously exacting when it came to execution. He paid attention to the smallest product details, from the font on the user interface to the packaging design. This fusion of big-picture thinking and detail-oriented follow-through resulted in breakthrough products like the iPhone, which revolutionised an entire industry.

The Intrepid Leader

How can you develop that balanced approach in your own leadership. Start by articulating your vision in clear terms. Know exactly what you want your organisation, project, or team to achieve. You should be able to explain it in simple language without resorting to jargon. If your statement of purpose is muddled, your team will struggle to rally around it. Once you have clarity, ensure that your team members also understand the "why" behind the vision. When people see the deeper reason for a goal, they commit with more enthusiasm.

After establishing the vision, switch gears to practical steps. Break down your grand objective into smaller tasks, objectives, or milestones. This is where execution begins. You might set weekly or monthly targets that your team can track. Assign responsibilities so that each individual knows their role. Keep an open line of communication to confirm that everyone's progress aligns with the broader plan. If your vision is like a lighthouse guiding the team, these smaller tasks are the stepping stones toward the shore.

It is vital to remain flexible. Your vision can remain steady, but the methods to achieve it might shift. If an approach fails, adjust and move on swiftly. Listen to data and feedback from the front lines. Many projects derail because a leader clings too tightly to a particular plan, ignoring indicators that it will not succeed. Adaptation is not surrender. It is the hallmark of a leader who prioritises outcomes over personal pride.

An often overlooked element of execution is accountability. Have the courage to measure your progress honestly. Establish key performance metrics that give you a clear picture of what is working and what is not. This data-driven mindset helps you pivot intelligently rather than making blind guesses about the source of a shortfall. However, do not let metrics overshadow the human side of leadership. Recognise the efforts of individuals, celebrate milestones, and tackle shortfalls by learning from them rather than punishing them.

Some organisations run into the trap of spending too long in the vision stage, obsessing over lofty goals, big presentations, and theoretical models. Others make the mistake of plunging into execution without a cohesive sense of purpose. Aim for the middle ground. Spark your people's imaginations with a bold view of the future, then ground them in the daily processes that move them closer to it. This balanced method fosters both innovation and productivity.

When vision and execution operate in harmony, you create momentum that can overcome obstacles and adapt to changing circumstances. You also build trust both within your team and with stakeholders who see tangible results. People are motivated when they witness real progress, but they are also inspired by a grander outlook that resonates with their own aspirations and values. That unity of purpose and practice is the mark of a leader who can rally others behind a meaningful cause and deliver lasting impact.

Conclusion

You have begun to refine the mental frameworks that elevate a person from a mere figurehead to a truly influential leader. The difference between bosses and leaders highlights the importance of service, empathy, and genuine accountability. The paradox of power underscores how humility can amplify your authority by inviting input and trust. The growth mindset encourages continuous learning and open-mindedness in a rapidly changing world. Building resilience ensures that you confront failure with the resolve of a warrior, turning every setback into an opportunity for growth. Finally, the delicate dance between vision and execution shows you how to transform big ideas into concrete results.

Each of these concepts shapes the way you think about and react to the challenges of leadership. They act as internal guides that inform your decisions and actions, even when external circumstances feel chaotic. You might meet doubters or face obstacles that appear insurmountable, but if your mindset remains anchored in these principles, you will maintain the composure and adaptability to press forward.

Moving ahead, you will discover how to apply these mental tools in more demanding scenarios. You have established a leadership mindset that is marked by integrity, humility, and a growth-oriented perspective. Your next task is to turn these mental pillars into lived realities, both in your daily interactions and in high-pressure environments. Keep pushing the boundaries of your thinking, and you will be ready for the leadership challenges on the horizon. The journey continues in the next chapter, where your ability to influence and motivate others will gain new depth.

CHAPTER 3

The Art Of Influence: How To Earn Respect And Trust

You have shaped your mindset and embraced the fundamentals of self-leadership. Now, you stand at the threshold of a skill that sets true leaders apart: influence. In a world flooded with shallow slogans and quick-fix approaches, genuine influence is the power to move people's hearts and minds without resorting to force or manipulation. It flows from your character, your actions, and the respect you earn rather than the authority you wield.

You are about to explore why authentic leadership is built on service to others. You will examine the power of giving before you expect anything in return, how deep listening can alter the course of an entire organisation, and the vital role that a consistent track record plays in forging a reputation that cannot be toppled by rumours or setbacks. You will also delve into the persuasive techniques that allow you to guide others toward shared success without compromising anyone's integrity. When you master these principles, you become a catalyst for growth and harmony. People trust your words and follow your direction, not because they must, but because they want to. That is the essence of influence. Let this chapter sharpen your capacity to inspire, unite, and uplift those who walk alongside you.

1. Why Leadership is About Service, Not Control

You might look at famous captains of industry or heads of state and imagine that leadership revolves around command and control. The reality is far different. True leadership is founded on a mindset of service. When you place your team's development, well-being, and progression at the forefront of your priorities, you create a current of loyalty and shared commitment that no enforced authority can match.

An example comes from the world of American football. Tony Dungy, the first black head coach to win a Super Bowl, credits his success to a philosophy that put players' personal growth on the same level as winning games. He listened to their stories, got to know their families, and motivated them to excel not just on the field but in life. This approach did not weaken his leadership. It gave him a squad of athletes who were willing to push beyond their own limits because they believed in his vision and, more importantly, felt that he believed in them.

When you dedicate yourself to serving others, you do more than hand out rewards. You guide people toward their best selves and equip them with the skills and mindset they need to flourish. A leader who builds this culture often sees longer retention, improved collaboration, and fewer internal conflicts because everyone understands that they are valued. They realise that their leader's success is tied to the collective progress of the entire group.

Serving does not mean spoiling. It means helping your people reach tough goals by clearing obstacles, offering resources, and delivering honest feedback. You set high standards and expect every individual to bring their best. Yet you do not motivate them through intimidation or empty threats. You achieve buy-in because your team senses that their leader is committed to their advancement. Your willingness to roll up your sleeves during a crisis further cements their respect.

Various reports from the Chartered Management Institute in the UK highlight that leaders who adopt a service mindset tend to foster organisational cultures of higher engagement and trust. In these environments, employees are more inclined to propose innovative ideas, raise concerns early, and assist peers who might be struggling. This tight-knit dynamic emerges naturally when people see that leadership is not fixated on control or ego.

Shifting your focus from control to service also refines your emotional intelligence. You start noticing subtle cues when someone on the team is stressed or at risk of burnout. You sense when morale is dipping and step in to investigate root causes rather than silencing complaints. This heightened empathy means you can offer solutions and guidance before issues spiral out of control. A domineering boss might overlook such cues, preoccupied with chasing targets above all else.

By serving, you ultimately wield a deeper form of influence. When you promote a team member, you do so because they have proven themselves ready, not because it suits a political agenda. When you correct mistakes, you do it with the sole aim of helping your people improve. Every action is geared toward collective success, and that authenticity resonates. People can spot a self-serving leader from a mile away, just as they can recognise one who puts their team above personal gain.

You might be wondering whether this service-based approach leaves room for tough decisions or discipline. Yes, it does. At times, you might have to let someone go if they consistently fail to meet standards or harm the group's harmony. The difference is that you handle those situations with fairness and transparency. You give feedback and opportunities to adapt, and if the final call is termination, it is executed with clarity and respect. You are not swinging an axe to prove who is in charge, you are acting on behalf of the team's greater good.

Ultimately, leadership built on service is resilient. It does not crumble if your title changes or if you lose formal authority. People follow you because they value your guidance and trust your motives. By choosing to serve, you ignite a profound loyalty that can see you through volatile market conditions, tight deadlines, and unexpected obstacles. This is the kind of influence that endures.

2. The Law of Reciprocity: Give Before You Expect

Influence often hinges on an unspoken rule that has guided human interaction for centuries. Researchers refer to it as reciprocity: the tendency for people to respond in kind when someone does something beneficial for them. You might recognise it as "I scratch your back, you scratch mine." Yet, when harnessed ethically, it becomes a powerful leadership tool that goes far beyond transactional exchanges.

Robert Cialdini, in his study of persuasion and social psychology, revealed that people feel a strong obligation to return favours, gifts, or kindnesses. That does not mean you hand out empty freebies hoping to manipulate others. Ethical use of reciprocity means you offer genuine support, valuable insights, or a helping hand without strings attached. This generosity builds goodwill, making others more open to your ideas and more inclined to assist you in return. Genuine generosity creates a cycle of mutual benefit rather than a one-sided arrangement.

The Art Of Influence: How To Earn Respect And Trust

Picture yourself as a project manager tackling a complex assignment. Deadlines are tight, and stakes are high. You notice a colleague struggling with a particular task that falls under your expertise. Instead of ignoring them to focus solely on your own responsibilities, you step in to guide them. You share your resources, your knowledge, and possibly a bit of your time. Initially, this might look like you are adding to your own workload. Yet your gesture fosters a spirit of collaboration. When your department faces a crunch, that same colleague will likely remember your support and come forward to lighten your load. This back-and-forth exchange allows the team to achieve goals that would be impossible in an environment of self-preservation.

Studies from the Ken Blanchard Companies suggest that leaders who practise giving before expecting see stronger interpersonal bonds and higher morale. Their findings show that employees in these settings become more cooperative and more likely to share ideas that can boost innovation. Instead of hoarding knowledge or playing political games, they feel encouraged to contribute for the greater good. The outcome is a culture of reciprocity where everyone is prepared to lend a hand because they trust that help will flow both ways.

You might worry about being exploited if you give too freely. This concern can be addressed by maintaining clear boundaries. Reciprocity is not about letting others walk all over you. It is about placing value on collaboration and goodwill while standing firm against those who consistently take without giving back. If you notice someone repeatedly capitalising on your help without contributing anything in return, address the issue. Offer them the chance to balance the scales. If they refuse, then you know to be more cautious in future interactions. The essence of reciprocity is mutual benefit, and if there is no mutual component, it becomes one-sided charity rather than a leadership strategy.

Reciprocity can also extend to intangible offerings like recognition, praise, or moral support. When you publicly recognise a teammate's hard work, you are effectively giving them appreciation. They are likely to become more enthusiastic about supporting your next idea or project. Positive energy bounces around the team, creating a healthier environment. That might sound fluffy, but it has real consequences for productivity and loyalty.

You can incorporate reciprocity into daily routines. Maybe you start your day by emailing a useful article to a colleague who is grappling with a particular challenge. Perhaps you invite an industry contact to speak at your company's event, introducing them to a new network of potential clients. Even small gestures, like staying late one night to help a team member complete a vital task, can strengthen bonds more than any formal directive. The shared trust that emerges from these acts of goodwill is more robust than any contract.

The law of reciprocity stands as a reminder that influence is not about seizing control or forcing compliance. It is about creating relationships where people are delighted to cooperate because they know you have their back. When everyone in your circle commits to giving before expecting, you establish a culture of respect and reliability. That culture will power your organisation through hardships and elevate your ability to persuade and unify those around you.

3. The Power of Listening: How to Lead Without Speaking

When people think of influential leaders, they often imagine stirring speeches or confident statements. Yet the most underrated quality of any leader is the ability to remain silent, pay attention, and truly hear what others have to say. Active listening can transform your leadership from top-down commands into a dynamic exchange of insights that propel your team forward.

Legendary basketball coach John Wooden, who steered the UCLA Bruins to numerous championships, was known for his measured demeanour and deliberate questions. He often remained silent while his players or assistant coaches spoke. This gave them space to express concerns, propose ideas, or identify challenges. By listening more than he spoke, Wooden captured crucial insights he might have missed if he was always in lecture mode. His approach created a sense of trust and collaboration, spurring his team to extraordinary success.

Effective listening begins with controlling your own urge to interrupt or formulate rebuttals. This might be difficult if you are used to leading from the front. Leaders are often expected to have ready solutions, yet sometimes your best move is to stand back and let the other person's point of view unfold. That process can reveal hidden issues, innovative ideas, or simmering resentments that would otherwise remain locked behind polite smiles.

Next, show genuine curiosity about the speaker's perspective. Maintain eye contact, ask clarifying questions, and resist any temptation to check your phone or glance at the clock. These might look like trivial details, but they communicate volumes about your respect for the other person's viewpoint. If they sense you are merely pretending to listen, they will shut down. If they feel your authentic interest, they will open up and share more nuanced observations.

You can strengthen your team's culture by incorporating structured listening sessions. For instance, schedule a short one-to-one every fortnight where you do more listening than talking. Let the team member set the agenda and focus on topics they find pressing. Encourage them to discuss roadblocks, resource constraints, or personal goals. If you listen actively, you can often catch problems early. Research from the Chartered Institute of Personnel and Development suggests that early conflict resolution can save up to 50 percent of the time and cost otherwise spent on damage control. These findings reflect the value of proactive listening as a management strategy.

Attentive leaders also notice non-verbal cues. Tone of voice, facial expressions, or nervous fidgeting might signal deeper issues. For instance, if a typically confident individual keeps their eyes down and speaks softly, it could point to feelings of doubt or fear. By tuning in, you can address those emotions, boosting morale before it spirals. This skill may appear subtle, yet it can make an immediate impact on how respected and supported your team feels.

Another advantage of strong listening is the example you set for your peers. When team members see their leader asking questions and taking notes, they learn that they should pay attention to one another. This can reduce office politics and cliques because open discussion becomes the norm rather than the exception. People feel valued, so they give their best and return that respect to others.

Finally, listening builds your credibility. If you speak up only after you have gathered enough information, your words carry greater weight. People understand that your input is well-considered and balanced. By contrast, the leader who fires off quick opinions without proper understanding erodes trust.

Over time, the team's respect for that leader diminishes. When you have a reputation for measured judgment, your influence goes far beyond hierarchical authority.

By harnessing the power of listening, you prove that influence is not always about commanding the spotlight. Sometimes, it is about giving the spotlight to others, letting them share their knowledge, ideas, and concerns. In doing so, you expand your own awareness and strengthen the bonds that unite your group. This quiet approach to leadership can unlock perspectives that a more forceful style might overlook, giving you a competitive edge in problem-solving and innovation.

4. Building an Unshakable Reputation Through Consistency

Your reputation is the bedrock of your influence, yet it cannot be established overnight. Leaders who say one thing and do another might win temporary applause, but they soon lose the faith of their followers. Real authority comes from consistent words and actions, day after day, especially when the spotlight is off and no one is applauding.

Jack Welch, the former CEO of General Electric, is remembered for consistently driving a culture of performance and accountability across all levels. Whether you agreed with his methods or not, he made no secret of his expectations and the reasons behind them. He implemented policies that held managers to rigorous standards, and he followed the same rules himself. His unwavering approach to performance left little space for confusion or hypocrisy. People knew exactly where he stood, which built a certain level of trust. That trust gave him immense influence and positioned GE as a global powerhouse for much of his tenure.

Consistency begins with clarity. You must know your principles, goals, and the limits you are not willing to cross. Spell them out to your team so they grasp where you stand. If integrity matters to you, make it plain in both words and actions. If punctuality is a core expectation, arrive early to meetings and enforce the standard across the board. If you preach open communication, maintain an open door and encourage others to discuss issues openly. Clear standards and transparent behaviour become a blueprint for your daily leadership.

When your actions match your statements, you form a foundation of trust that is difficult to dismantle. Even if your decisions are unpopular at times, people will often respect you for standing by your word. On the other hand, if you flip-flop when the winds change, you erode your reliability. That erosion will spread through your team, creating doubt about your ability to navigate future challenges.

A CIPD study focused on employee engagement found that teams led by consistent leaders showed higher levels of cooperation and stronger alignment with organisational goals. This is not surprising. When guidelines do not shift randomly, people feel safe investing in shared objectives. They are also more inclined to speak up when something is off because they trust the environment is stable enough to handle honest dialogue. Consistency sets the tone for an environment where everyone can focus on performance instead of second-guessing leadership's sincerity.

Another component of reputation is how you treat individuals when they stumble. If you claim to support growth and development, you must back it up when a team member fails. Offer resources or coaching rather than immediate punishment if the individual shows the will to improve. This balanced response signals that you genuinely believe in helping people evolve. It also showcases your consistency between the values you proclaim and the actions you take.

Of course, no leader is infallible. You might slip occasionally or need to revise a policy if circumstances drastically change. The key is owning those moments. Announce your reasons, apologise if needed, and outline the path forward. Leaders who pretend they did not shift course destroy their own credibility. By demonstrating honesty about your adjustments, you preserve respect.

Lastly, be patient. Building an unshakable reputation requires time, especially if your environment has seen inconsistent leadership in the past. People might initially be cautious or sceptical. Prove your stability step by step, handling both victories and setbacks with the same measured approach. Over the long haul, this reliability becomes part of your personal brand. As your reputation solidifies, your words will carry more weight, and you will gain the trust of colleagues, subordinates, and even those in senior positions.

In a world where public perception can swing wildly with every social media post, a consistent leader stands out as an anchor of reliability. While others chase quick approval, you remain steadfast in your principles. This is not always the fastest path to popularity, but it is the surest path to respect and lasting influence. When you want to mobilise people toward a vision, they will follow someone they know they can rely on. This reliability is the hallmark of an unshakable reputation.

5. The Science of Persuasion: How to Move People Without Forcing Them

Persuasion is not a shady trick. It is the art of guiding people toward a choice that benefits everyone involved. True persuasion neither twists arms nor conceals agendas. Instead, it aligns individual motivations, creates a sense of shared gain, and fosters genuine buy-in. Great leaders understand that forcing compliance breeds resentment, while respectful persuasion builds loyalty.

Military leader and statesman Dwight D. Eisenhower once remarked that leadership is the art of getting someone else to do something you want done because they want to do it. When he served as Supreme Allied Commander during World War II, Eisenhower had to coordinate forces from multiple nations, each with their own interests and command structures. He could not bully allied generals into adopting his strategies; he had to persuade them by outlining the benefits of unity and focusing on shared goals. This collaborative strategy laid the groundwork for a successful alliance that overcame massive obstacles.

Modern research into the science of persuasion reveals several core principles. One is social proof: people often look at what their peers or trusted individuals are doing before deciding how to act. Another is commitment and consistency: once someone publicly commits to an idea, they are more likely to follow through. For instance, if team members voice support for a new training program in a meeting, they will feel more compelled to complete it later. A third principle is scarcity: when a resource or opportunity is limited, people value it more. If you highlight that a certain role or chance is rare, individuals might feel a stronger urge to seize it.

However, these principles must be handled with ethical care. Manipulating emotions or hiding important details can backfire spectacularly. People who feel tricked will lose trust and might retaliate by disengaging or undermining your goals. Ethical persuasion means stating facts clearly, allowing space for questions or concerns, and being transparent about potential downsides. This method might slow down the decision-making process, but it lays a stable foundation for collective commitment.

Skilful persuasion also involves speaking in terms that resonate with your audience's interests. Suppose you want your team to embrace a new software platform. Instead of issuing an abrupt mandate, explain how it will save each person time, reduce errors, or add to their career skill set. If you want senior stakeholders to invest in fresh technology, demonstrate the return on investment. Show them data or credible case studies. The idea is to connect the change you are proposing with a direct benefit to those who must implement it.

Active involvement further strengthens persuasion. If you involve your team in planning or testing a new project, they take ownership of it. Their input shapes the final product, so they feel more inclined to see it succeed. This contrasts sharply with a scenario where you simply impose a solution from the top without explanation. Research from the Centre for Management and Organisation Effectiveness has shown that people who co-create solutions are more satisfied with the outcome and show greater long-term commitment.

Emotions also play a role in persuasion. A leader who speaks passionately about a vision and demonstrates how it can positively impact everyone's future often gains traction faster than one who simply rattles off data. Nevertheless, passion must be grounded in substance. If you rely solely on hype, you risk disappointment once the initial excitement fades.

Balance logical arguments with emotional appeal to create a persuasive message that stands up to scrutiny.

Finally, remember that persuasion is a two-way street. Listen to feedback and remain open to refining your proposal. If people sense that you are genuinely willing to adjust based on their insights, they feel respected and are more likely to support you. This respectful approach fosters a deeper level of commitment, which is vital for turning ideas into reality. Through ethical persuasion, you transform potential naysayers into motivated allies and temporary collaborators into lasting partners.

Conclusion

Influence is the lifeblood of effective leadership, yet it does not rest on formal titles or the power to punish. It is rooted in how you serve, what you contribute, how intently you listen, and whether you stand by your words when no one else is looking. You have seen why genuine service to your team inspires loyalty far beyond what a controlling attitude can ever achieve. You have discovered how giving before you expect becomes a golden rule that fuels collaboration. You have learned that leadership without active listening is a weak imitation of true influence, and you have looked into the building blocks of a reputation that remains solid under scrutiny.

You have also dived into the science behind persuasion, learning that honest, respectful methods resonate far more than brute force. Taken together, these lessons show that influence is not a trick or an accident. It is a craft you develop through self-awareness, ethical principles, and daily practice. Leaders who excel in these areas do more than command teams. They earn genuine trust and inspire people to reach for objectives that once seemed out of reach.

Let these insights guide the next stage of your leadership evolution. Combine them with the foundations and mindset you have already cultivated. Refine your character, practise generosity, grow your emotional intelligence, and refine your approach to persuasion. The path ahead may involve challenges, but you will face them from a position of strength. You now know how to rally individuals around a shared purpose, sustain their respect, and keep your integrity intact while you do it. That is the art of influence at its best, and you are ready to wield it with honour.

CHAPTER 4

Leadership In Action: Decision-Making Under Pressure

You have laid a solid foundation by leading yourself, adopting a strong leadership mindset, and mastering the art of influence. Now comes the practical test of real-world leadership: making tough decisions swiftly and effectively, especially when the stakes are high. It is one thing to formulate grand visions or speak eloquently about principles. It is quite another to stand in the heat of the moment, gather your courage, and choose a path that may well define your legacy. This is where leadership becomes action, not theory.

In this chapter, you will learn why you must never wait for perfect information before you act, how courage can outweigh comfort when you face daunting crossroads and the value of balancing instinct with hard data. You will gain insights into calculating risks without paralysing yourself or your team. Finally, you will see that great leaders are not afraid to own up to their mistakes. If you can humbly change course when you realise you are wrong, you transform a stumble into a teaching moment. Every section in this chapter is designed to sharpen your decision-making under pressure so that you can guide your team through chaos with calm resolve.

1. The 70% Rule: Why Perfect Decisions Don't Exist

Leadership In Action: Decision-Making Under Pressure

When you find yourself in a crisis, you might wait for the stars to align before making a choice, hoping for complete certainty. Yet waiting for perfect information is usually a losing strategy. As time ticks away, fresh complications arise, and opportunities slip through your fingers. Leadership often means seizing the initiative when you have "good enough" information rather than exhaustive data that may never arrive.

A guiding principle shared by numerous military strategists and business innovators is sometimes referred to as the 70% Rule. Although different leaders phrase it differently, the essence is the same: once you have around 70% of the facts you think you need, you ought to act. If you wait until you are 100% sure, you might miss the moment when your decision could have the most impact. This approach is not reckless. It acknowledges that waiting indefinitely can be just as dangerous as making a hasty and uninformed choice.

General Colin Powell famously advised that leaders should make decisions when they have between 40% and 70% of the information needed. Under 40%, you are gambling. Over 70%, you may be stalling. Although Powell's experiences are often cited in American contexts, the logic is universal. Decisions made quickly, based on enough intelligence to form a reasoned plan, give you a head start in implementing and adapting to unforeseen developments. You avoid being stuck in the analysis loop, where fear of imperfection leads to crippling indecision.

In modern business environments, an example of this principle can be seen in Spotify's continual rollout of new features. The company does not wait until every potential glitch is ironed out. Instead, it launches updates on a rolling basis, then refines them in response to user feedback. If Spotify waited for a perfect release, it would risk losing ground to competitors launching faster. This real-time adaptation underscores the power of moving with incomplete data rather than seeking flawless certainty.

Psychologically, perfectionism can derail good leadership. You might fear the embarrassment of a wrong call, so you linger in never-ending fact-finding. But time is a resource you cannot replenish. Each day spent in paralysis is a day that customers, rivals, or other forces move ahead. The pursuit of an error-free decision can be more harmful than making a strong move and adjusting as circumstances evolve. Accepting that you will never know everything fosters a proactive spirit that sees mistakes as correctable, not catastrophic.

Adopting the 70% Rule also demands that you trust your team. If everyone is paralysed, waiting for you to decree the ideal plan, progress halts. Instead, you can delegate certain tasks or allow knowledgeable team members to make judgement calls, empowering them to act quickly with partial information. This approach not only speeds up processes but also keeps morale high by showing that you respect their expertise. The key is to establish a framework of accountability so that if something goes awry, the team can pivot rather than point fingers.

Yet, this does not mean rushing blindly. Gathering data still matters, especially the crucial facts that set your direction. The 70% Rule is about deciding when you have enough insights to form a sensible plan. You work with that plan and adapt as new information surfaces. If you realise you have marched down the wrong path, you adjust and carry on. That method spares you the regret of having done nothing at all.

Ultimately, the idea that perfect decisions do not exist frees you to act with boldness. You accept that part of leadership is venturing into unknowns and making the best call you can with the available intelligence. The true failure is not in choosing an imperfect course but in refusing to choose at all. By applying the 70% Rule in your daily life, you convert hesitation into momentum. You drive projects forward and instil a culture of adaptive thinking, proving to your team that speed and agility can often trump the elusive chase for perfection.

2. Courage Over Comfort: Making Hard Choices

You will confront decisions that unsettle you to the core. Perhaps it involves cutting a project that shows personal promise but no longer serves the greater mission. Maybe you have to dismiss a friend who is underperforming or pivot away from a product line that has been part of your organisation's identity for years. When these crossroads appear, choosing comfort might keep you liked or help you avoid immediate pain, but it can destroy the long-term interests of your group. Great leaders stand firm and pick the harder path if it advances the greater good.

Margaret Thatcher, who served as Prime Minister of the United Kingdom during a turbulent economic era, often spoke about having to make difficult decisions that sparked resistance. She pushed forward with policies that she believed would revive the British economy, even though they caused short-term upheaval and invited fierce criticism. Whether one agrees with her policies or not, her commitment to courage over comfort remains an illustration of leadership under fire. She decided that it was better to act decisively than to shy away from controversy, and her decisions reshaped Britain's economic landscape for decades.

In your environment, you might not be dealing with national policy. Yet, you still face pivotal moments where going along with the status quo seems safer than challenging it. If your team is failing to meet targets, it could be tempting to relax standards to keep everyone content. Instead, a courageous leader will address the issues head-on, even if that risks temporary disapproval or conflict. In time, people respect the leader who acts with principle far more than the one who bends to keep everyone happy.

Courage in decision-making does not equal blunt force or reckless confrontation. It requires clear-eyed realism and a willingness to weigh the consequences of both action and inaction. You do not step forward blindly. You study the scenario, gather insights, and plan for likely outcomes. Yet, once you see that the tough choice is the correct one, you do not shrink back to preserve your comfort. You move ahead, knowing you might face backlash or personal discomfort along the way.

A significant factor in building courage is clarity of purpose. When you are grounded in a well-defined mission, you have a beacon that guides you through the fog of doubt. If your guiding principle is restoring honesty or raising performance standards, you make decisions consistent with that principle. Aligning your actions with a higher cause or a set of values gives you the moral and emotional reserves to withstand criticism. Without that clarity, courage can waver the moment tension rises.

Another driver of courage is accepting that leadership inevitably comes with hard calls. There is no realm of responsibility where you will always be thanked for every move. If you chase universal approval, you forfeit genuine leadership. You may attempt to please everyone only to end up pleasing no one. When you embrace the reality that tough decisions are part of your duty, you strip away the unrealistic desire to remain universally popular. That acceptance frees you to do what must be done.

Cultivating courage also means learning how to handle the stress and potential loneliness that may result from an unpopular decision. Stress management, whether through reflection, physical exercise, or trusted mentorship, is crucial. You need these outlets to remain strong enough to deal with your own doubts. If you stand alone too long without support, your resolve can weaken. Seek counsel from mentors who have walked a similar road, but remember that the final accountability rests with you.

Your team, and indeed your organisation, will look to you for signals on how to handle adversity. If you demonstrate that you are unafraid to make the tough call, you teach them to confront challenges directly. You also set a standard for integrity, showing that expediency does not trump ethics or the broader mission. In the end, choosing courage over comfort might cost you in the short run, but it carves out the path that leads to long-term respect. People might not always like your decisions, yet they will learn to trust your resolve and the consistency of your moral compass. That trust is the backbone of enduring leadership.

3. The Role of Instinct vs. Data in Leadership

Modern leadership often involves a tug-of-war between instinct and data. With endless spreadsheets, analytics dashboards, and algorithms at your disposal, you might think every dilemma has a purely numerical solution. Yet ignore your intuition at your peril. Some of history's transformative decisions were the product of a leader's gut feeling, refined by experience and insight. The best leaders learn to combine both: they interpret relevant data while trusting their inner compass to guide the final call.

Elon Musk's rise with SpaceX and Tesla demonstrates this balancing act. While both ventures rely on rigorous data, engineering calculations, simulation models, safety protocols, Musk has repeatedly trusted his instinct to push boundaries. SpaceX pursued vertical landings of rocket boosters against the advice of industry veterans, who believed the idea too costly and prone to failure. Had Musk followed purely conservative data projections, he might have avoided those attempts altogether. His instincts drove him to persist. Over multiple failed landings, the engineering team fine-tuned the process until they succeeded. Today, those reusable rockets have revolutionised cost efficiency in space travel.

That example highlights why leaders need more than a calculator. Data can indicate whether a plan is feasible, but it rarely captures intangible elements like team morale, competitor psychology, or the subtle shifts in consumer sentiment. Intuition, shaped by experience and emotional intelligence, can detect signals that pure statistics overlook. Yet relying solely on gut instincts without verifying them can lead to wild decisions that backfire.

You can strike a healthy balance by first clarifying your objectives. If your primary goal is to expand into a new market, gather pertinent data: potential profit margins, competitor positioning, local regulations. This information forms the backbone of your strategic approach. Then, interrogate your instincts. What do they tell you about that region's cultural mindset or about your organisation's readiness to handle the expansion. Ask yourself if you sense deeper risks or opportunities that the data does not reveal.

Leadership In Action: Decision-Making Under Pressure

Discuss these hunches with trusted colleagues who can offer alternative viewpoints.

It is also crucial to refine your instincts through continuous learning. Your instincts become sharper as your knowledge base expands. When you begin in a new field, your intuition may be underdeveloped. As you accumulate lessons from successes and failures, your gut feeling becomes more reliable. That is why seasoned leaders often spot pitfalls that younger counterparts miss. Their instincts have been tempered by hard-won experience.

However, do not confuse stubbornness with intuition. If multiple pieces of evidence contradict your gut feeling, be willing to investigate further. Pride can masquerade as instinct, prompting you to dismiss every fact that conflicts with your cherished view. Healthy intuition remains open to revision when confronted with strong contrary data. You are aiming for the sweet spot where logic and feeling work in tandem.

Emerging research from management scientists at the University of Reading indicates that effective decision-makers integrate emotional awareness with analytical results. In their studies, leaders who scored high on emotional intelligence and who also utilised concrete data produced stronger outcomes than those who relied on just one of the two. The synergy is the key: neither pure data nor raw instinct alone is enough. Each informs the other.

In the modern digital age, you have more data than ever. The challenge is not a lack of information but an overabundance. Sifting through this sea of numbers to find relevant insights is itself a skill. Once you have that short list of essential metrics, you must still interpret them within context. This is where your intuition steps in. If data suggests a product line is profitable, yet your instincts sense a shifting market mood, proceed with caution or pivot. If statistics warn of risk, but your gut and real-world observations hint at a potential breakthrough, you might choose to go against the grain.

Ultimately, whether you are pioneering new technology or leading a local volunteer group, the most vital skill is knowing when to trust your instincts and when to lean on data. If you learn to balance the two, you gain the flexibility to seize unexpected openings while avoiding reckless leaps in the dark. This dual approach sets you apart as a leader who is not just knowledgeable but also adept at reading the undercurrents that raw numbers cannot always measure.

4. Risk-Taking: When to Be Bold, When to Be Cautious

Risk is inseparable from leadership. In every significant decision, there is a chance of failure. Yet growth seldom happens in the comfort zone. Leaders who hope to excel must decide when to push boundaries and when to hold back. Mastering that balance can be the difference between explosive success and a costly catastrophe.

Jeff Bezos, founder of Amazon, popularised a concept known as "Type 1" and "Type 2" decisions. Type 1 decisions are irreversible. Once made, the consequences are huge and changing course might be extremely difficult. Type 2 decisions can be reversed if they go wrong. By categorising decisions in this manner, Bezos encourages leaders to take bold risks on Type 2 items, where the fallout is manageable. Meanwhile, Type 1 decisions demand more caution, deeper analysis, and potentially a slower pace. This structure helps you allocate your risk-taking energy wisely.

Before charging ahead, define the potential outcomes. If you are preparing to launch a new product, what might you gain if it succeeds, and what is the worst-case scenario if it flops. Be realistic and thorough. This does not mean you are succumbing to fear. You are simply acknowledging the stakes so that you can make a clear-eyed judgement. Sometimes, a high-reward opportunity might come with a manageable downside. That is the green light to be bold. Other times, the payoff might be too small to justify the potential harm. Being cautious then becomes the wiser route.

Timing also plays a crucial role in risk-taking. A plan that is risky now might be safer in a few months once resources, team skills, or market conditions improve. Equally, waiting too long for perfect timing could mean missing the ideal window. An example is Netflix's pivot from DVD rentals to streaming services back in 2007. The move was bold because internet speeds were not universally high, and physical rentals still dominated. Yet the Netflix leadership believed that streaming would soon reshape the industry, so they took the leap early. Competitors who waited for more obvious signs ended up trailing in market share. Netflix gained a head start that proved decisive.

Financial stability is another factor. If your cash reserves are thin, a high-stakes gamble can bankrupt your enterprise, leaving no chance for recovery. On the other hand, if you have a robust safety net, you can afford to invest in experiments that might fail. This principle does not only apply to corporations. Even in smaller outfits, it matters whether you have the time, budget, and morale to withstand a potential misstep. Risk tolerance often aligns with how resilient you are to short-term setbacks.

Cultural acceptance of risk in your organisation is just as important. If your workplace punishes every failure harshly, people will shy away from bold decisions. As a leader, you can create a balanced environment where measured gambles are encouraged, provided they are underpinned by logic and a contingency plan. If the outcome is negative, you dissect the lessons rather than point fingers. Over time, your team becomes more comfortable taking strategic risks, which spawns creativity and innovation.

Be mindful not to mistake rashness for boldness. True boldness involves a calculated approach: you know the stakes, you weigh possibilities, and you decide that the potential upside is worth the exposure. Recklessness ignores warning signs and forges ahead on gut feeling alone. That is not leadership; it is a dice roll.

In the end, deciding when to be bold and when to be cautious is one of the most nuanced tasks of leadership. You will not always get it right. Even the most carefully analysed risk can unravel due to unforeseen developments. Yet, if you build a culture that supports calculated gambles and swift recovery from errors, you unleash a powerful momentum. Over time, those who master this balance establish a track record of successful ventures that elevate them from ordinary managers to visionary leaders. They inspire trust because they are neither paralysed by fear nor blinded by reckless ambition.

5. Course Correction: Admitting When You're Wrong

Every leader, no matter how skilled, will eventually take a misstep. You might approve a product launch that flops spectacularly, make a hiring decision that undermines team morale, or back an initiative that drains resources without payoff. When that happens, your true leadership quality shines through in how you respond. Admitting you are wrong is not a sign of weakness. It is an act of authenticity that can salvage respect and prevent further damage.

Leadership In Action: Decision-Making Under Pressure

Toyota, long praised for quality, faced a major crisis in the late 2000s when reports of unintended acceleration resulted in recalls of millions of vehicles. Initial responses seemed defensive, which worsened public backlash. Once the company's leadership fully acknowledged the scale of the problem and owned up to it, Toyota pivoted. They implemented more stringent safety checks, improved internal communication, and overhauled their approach to transparency with consumers. That shift helped restore faith in the brand and demonstrated that an admission of error could lead to constructive change. Had Toyota continued to dodge responsibility, the organisation's reputation might have never recovered.

As a leader, stepping forward to say you were wrong dismantles fear within the team. People see that mistakes can be openly addressed, so they no longer hide errors or shift blame. This transparency accelerates problem-solving because issues are laid out in the open. You also position yourself as a human being rather than an untouchable authority figure. Your team feels more secure experimenting with new ideas, knowing that if things do not work out, the response will be honest reflection, not a witch-hunt.

Admitting a mistake does not mean stopping there. You need to outline how you will correct course. Suppose you launched a marketing campaign that failed to attract customers. You might acknowledge the error by explaining which assumptions proved false and how you plan to adjust in the next campaign. That second step, showing a clear plan of action, marks the difference between helpless regret and proactive growth. People want to see that you have learned from the slip and are guiding the group toward a better path.

This approach also sets an example for your subordinates. When they see you accept responsibility, they learn to do the same. That culture of responsibility can prevent toxic blame games and unhealthy silos. People focus on solutions rather than covering their tracks. In teams where the leader never admits fault, subordinates either learn to fear mistakes or hide them. In both scenarios, long-term damage to trust and productivity is almost certain.

You might worry that frequent admissions of error will erode your authority. In truth, you should not be making monumental misjudgements all the time. Regular reflection and well-informed decision-making can reduce that risk. Still, even the best leaders slip up occasionally. When it happens, an honest admission followed by swift corrective action typically strengthens your authority. Your team and your stakeholders see that you lead with integrity. They also see that you can pivot before a bad situation escalates into disaster.

In practical terms, be candid yet measured in your admission. State the nature of the error, explain what went awry, and keep any unnecessary drama out of it. Do not wallow in self-criticism, nor should you let others use your admission as a platform for personal attacks. A calm, direct explanation tells everyone you are serious about solutions and not interested in theatrics or scapegoating. If third parties, such as partners or customers, were harmed by your decisions, a sincere apology can be invaluable. People often forgive mistakes if they sense genuine regret and observe concrete steps to put things right.

Over the long run, your ability to recalibrate when you are wrong is a testament to your adaptability. Rigidity in the face of obvious failure leads to organisational stagnation, moral decay, and the eventual collapse of trust. By contrast, course correction keeps your team agile and fosters a sense of collective resilience. You all learn that a misstep is not fatal but can be a catalyst for improvement. When you own your errors with grace, you underscore the message that leadership is about steady progress rather than flawless performance.

Conclusion

Decision-making under pressure reveals your true measure as a leader. Throughout this chapter, you have discovered that waiting for perfect information can paralyse progress, that courageous decisions often come with personal discomfort, and that intuition and data are not competitors but partners in guiding your choices. You have also learned the nuanced art of risk-taking, recognising that timing, resource levels, and the nature of each choice demand a thoughtful blend of boldness and caution. Finally, you have seen that admitting when you are wrong requires humility but can salvage confidence and spark better outcomes.

These principles go beyond theory. They are the day-to-day tasks of anyone in a position of authority. By applying the 70% Rule, you stay agile and avoid letting perfectionism hold you back. By choosing courage over comfort, you embody the strength your team looks for when uncertainty looms. By harmonising instinct with data, you become both visionary and grounded. By balancing risk and caution, you turn challenges into calculated adventures. And by learning to course-correct, you prove that real leadership is an evolving path, not a static position.

Carry these ideas into your next high-stakes decision. Embrace them when the pressure mounts, and you must act swiftly. Integrate them into your leadership style so that your choices reflect consistency, clarity, and moral fortitude. In doing so, you equip yourself to guide your team through even the roughest waters. The chapters ahead will continue to push you further into the realities of leadership, demanding that you grow, adapt, and stand firm in the face of even greater trials. Keep these decision-making insights close at hand as you move forward. They will serve as your compass when the storm clouds gather, and your next move could define your ultimate legacy.

CHAPTER 5

The Warrior's Path: Strength, Honour, And Grit

Leadership is not a polite stroll through calm gardens. It is a path fraught with conflict, doubt, and the heavy weight of responsibility. In your quest to become a formidable leader, you must learn to walk this path like a warrior. Warriors do not merely talk about bold principles or recite stirring phrases. They forge their character in the heat of trials, finding the strength to persevere when everything seems to crumble. They stand by a code of honour that guides their decisions, even when shortcuts promise an easier life. And they learn to balance power with compassion, discovering that true might lies in uniting respect for oneself with empathy for others.

This chapter will guide you through five core concepts that shape the warrior's path. You will see why hardships do not signal failure but rather serve as the crucible that forms genuine leaders. You will study mental toughness as a tool to stay centred when chaos blindsides you. You will explore what it means to uphold a code of honour that transcends mere titles. You will also discover how real strength embraces compassion, turning might into a force for unity. Finally, you will confront your own inner demons: self-doubt, fear, and ego. By waging war on these internal obstacles, you will emerge with a deeper understanding of what it takes to lead with unwavering resolve. Each concept builds upon the last to forge you into a leader ready to charge forward with clarity and fortitude.

1. Why Every Great Leader Faces Trials and Hardships

In the cinematic portrayal of leadership, you often see charismatic figures marching triumphantly to the applause of admirers. Yet, real leadership is rarely so glamorous. Trials and hardships are not side effects; they are main events on the road to greatness. If you look across history, you will see that every influential leader has endured severe setbacks and crises. These moments are not random misfortunes but essential tests that separate those with hollow ambition from those who possess the grit to press on.

Horatio Nelson, one of Britain's most celebrated naval commanders, exemplified this reality. He lost sight in one eye early in his career and later lost an arm in battle. Despite these daunting obstacles, he led the Royal Navy to key victories through strategy, courage, and the unwavering belief that adversity was not an excuse to retreat. The hardships he faced at sea, ranging from injuries to ferocious storms, sharpened his determination. While physical losses may have dented his body, they crystallised his leadership, winning him loyalty from his sailors and admiration from a nation.

You might not be fighting in a literal naval battle, but you will still encounter fierce challenges. A significant project might collapse unexpectedly. A trusted ally might walk away when you need them most. A personal crisis might strike when you are on the brink of a career-defining pitch. These moments can feel like an ambush, pulling you away from the steady progress you thought you had under control. Yet, in truth, they offer you the chance to prove your resilience. When you stand resolute despite adversity, people learn to trust in your capacity. That trust fuels your ability to influence and lead.

Research from McKinsey & Company indicates that organisations led by individuals who have weathered significant hardships tend to display stronger adaptation skills in volatile markets. The reason is straightforward: Leaders who have learned lessons in crisis are more likely to anticipate future dangers. They do not wilt at the first sign of trouble because they have already endured painful disruptions. In your own realm, adversity might take different forms- economic downturns, internal conflicts, or technological failures- but your response carries more weight than the problem itself.

Hardships can also realign your priorities. When everything goes smoothly, you might become complacent or lose sight of your core mission. A major setback forces you to reflect on what truly matters. It compels you to strip away the superficial and focus on the fundamental values and objectives that should guide your decisions. If you use hardships to clarify your sense of purpose, you emerge with renewed focus that permeates your entire team.

Moreover, trials reveal your authenticity. It is easy to appear principled and focused when conditions are favourable. The true measure of your character emerges in the face of adversity. Do you stand by your ethical code when a corner-cutting opportunity could rescue your organisation from short-term loss. Do you maintain transparency with your team when it might be simpler to hide mistakes and shift the blame? Your answers to these questions define your legacy as a leader. Over time, those who remain honourable through hardships gain a reputation for reliability that is nearly impossible to undermine.

A crucial point is that you cannot dodge every challenge. Attempting to avoid hardships at all costs can cause more harm than good. Leaders who run from difficulties create an environment of denial. This stifles growth because no one learns to handle genuine obstacles. By facing trials head-on, you invite your colleagues to do the same. You foster a culture where facing problems, rather than burying them, becomes second nature. This culture of honest confrontation builds a collective resilience that amplifies your leadership efforts.

When you recognise that hardships are an integral chapter in every leadership story, you stop viewing them as catastrophic misfortunes. Instead, you embrace them as opportunities to test your mental toughness, refine your strategy, and deepen the trust of those around you. If you are in the midst of a trial right now, step up with boldness. Adapt your approach, recommit to your principles, and stand as a beacon for your team. In doing so, you will prove that adversity is not your downfall; it is your forge, shaping you into a leader truly worthy of the title.

2. Mental Toughness: How to Stay Strong in Chaos

Chaos arrives unannounced. It upends your tidy plans, rattles your confidence, and plunges your team into uncertainty. This is where mental toughness becomes your most valuable asset. Mental toughness is not about never feeling stress or fear. It is about forging an internal posture that enables you to remain calm, decisive, and forward-focused when the world around you falls into disarray.

Retired Navy officer David Marquet offers a striking demonstration of mental toughness. He was assigned to command a nuclear submarine, the USS Santa Fe, which had the worst performance record in the fleet. Determined to turn it around, Marquet introduced a leadership model that empowered crew members at every level to speak up and take responsibility. Challenges came thick and fast: technical issues, staff scepticism, and the deep-rooted culture of passivity. Maintaining composure under these pressures demanded a robust mental framework. Marquet's unwavering focus and belief in his crew's potential transformed the Santa Fe into one of the highest-rated submarines in the US Navy. That transformation depended on mental resilience in the face of relentless obstacles.

You do not need to command a submarine to see how chaos can spin your environment. An unexpected market shift might slash your revenue projections. A sudden loss of key personnel might derail an important project. Your mental toughness rests on your ability to manage emotional volatility, keep clarity of mind, and act on constructive solutions. The first step is acknowledging your stress. Pretending you are unaffected can lead to denial, which hinders swift action. By admitting that chaos has arrived, you gain the honesty required to tackle it effectively.

Techniques for cultivating mental toughness vary, but a consistent thread involves training your focus. One method is to practise controlled breathing. When chaos spikes, your body reacts with adrenaline, increasing your heart rate and tension. Deliberate, slow breaths lower the physical symptoms of stress. This steadies your mind, making it easier to sift through complex problems without succumbing to panic. Another approach is to break down large uncertainties into smaller, manageable tasks. Instead of allowing your brain to run in circles over a vast unknown, shift it to a short list of actionable steps. Completing even one small action can restore a sense of control.

Studies from the British Psychological Society suggest that leaders who build daily mental disciplines, like journaling challenges, engaging in mindfulness, or setting brief reflection periods, develop higher resilience in crises. These habits train your brain to adapt to sudden changes rather than crumble under them. If you maintain a routine of mental conditioning, you will find that you can bounce back from disruptive events more rapidly.

Resilient leaders also use self-talk effectively. You might catch yourself thinking, "This is impossible" or "I cannot handle this." Such negative internal chatter can become a self-fulfilling prophecy. By rephrasing your thoughts, "This is a significant challenge, but I have solved serious problems before", you direct your energy toward solutions rather than defeat. Repeatedly telling yourself that you have the resources to cope strengthens your belief and helps maintain composure in the face of turmoil.

Mental toughness further relies on perspective. In chaotic moments, it is easy to feel as if your entire world is collapsing. Step back and ask: how pivotal is this situation in the grand scheme. Has your team faced similar challenges previously. Are you overestimating the severity of potential losses. By putting problems into perspective, you stop them from ballooning out of proportion. This can reduce anxiety and free up bandwidth for strategic thinking.

Lastly, mental toughness is not an isolated trait. It thrives in supportive environments. Encourage your team to voice concerns openly and share ideas for solutions. If everyone feels they must hide anxiety, panic grows behind closed doors. Transparent communication allows you to spot genuine dangers and devise swift countermeasures. It also spreads a sense of unity, reminding everyone that they are not battling chaos alone.

In the end, mental toughness is your shield against the swirling forces of chaos. It enables you to remain steady when others falter, to adapt when circumstances shift, and to lead decisively when lesser minds freeze. This is not a gift reserved for a select few. It is a discipline you build day by day, crisis by crisis, until you can stand unshaken by the tempests that tear through ordinary leaders. Embrace it, practise it, and watch as you develop the rock-solid poise that characterises unbreakable leadership.

3. The Code of Honour: Leading with Integrity

Amid the world's shifting sands of convenience and compromise, you must anchor yourself in a code of honour if you aim to lead with enduring impact. Integrity forms the bedrock of this code. It is the unspoken promise you make to live by a set of principles that do not vanish under pressure or morph based on personal benefit. In an environment where cunning shortcuts can look tempting and double standards might pass unnoticed, standing firm in your code of honour sets you apart.

Historically, the ancient Samurai of Japan followed Bushido, a strict code centred on loyalty, courage, and moral righteousness. These warriors were formidable not just because of their martial skill but because their sense of honour dictated how they lived each day. They believed that betraying their code was worse than losing a battle. While you are unlikely to fight sword duels, the principle remains the same: A leader who upholds a personal code of honour earns unwavering respect and trust. Even your critics will acknowledge the clarity of your moral stance.

Living with integrity means your deeds match your declarations, regardless of audience or context. You treat your team with the same respect when they exceed targets and when they fall behind. You refuse to manipulate data or sugar-coat failures to look good in front of superiors. If an error occurs on your watch, you hold yourself accountable. Some might think such transparency exposes weakness, yet, in reality, it builds credibility. People learn that your word is reliable. Once they see that reliability, they give you the loyalty that only genuine respect can foster.

Practical leadership research from Warwick Business School has revealed that organisations with leaders known for high integrity experience lower employee turnover and higher engagement. Trust, once established through consistent moral conduct, removes a great deal of friction. Teams do not need to waste energy second-guessing motives or setting up defensive strategies. They can direct their full attention to performance and innovation because they know the leadership will not exploit them or shift goals unfairly.

One challenge, however, is that integrity often requires self-sacrifice. You might have to reject lucrative but unethical deals, or you might have to stand up for a team member when doing so could damage your standing with certain higher-ups. The short-term losses can sting, but in the long run, a leader who refuses to betray core values becomes a fortress of reliability. Competitors who rely on underhanded tactics might gain quick advantages, but they typically stumble when exposed, destroying trust among clients, partners, and employees.

Your code of honour must also address how you handle conflicts of interest. Imagine you are hiring for a key role, and a close friend seems eager to take it. If they lack the necessary competence, honour demands you do what is best for the organisation, not for your personal friendship. Such decisions might cause tension temporarily, but they protect the larger mission. By consistently selecting fairness over bias, you confirm that no one person's preference overrides the collective good.

Clarity is essential. Write down your core principles or declare them publicly. This may sound old-fashioned, but it cements your commitment and allows your team to understand what you stand for. Do you prioritise honesty, loyalty, or transparency above all else. Do you promise to accept accountability for mistakes. Articulate these vows in a concise manner. Then lead by them. Actions speak louder than empty slogans, and your consistency will be tested the moment real pressures arise.

Another hidden benefit of a clear code of honour is that it simplifies decision-making. In morally grey areas, you have a guiding compass that tells you which direction to follow. This spares you from agonising each time an ethical dilemma surfaces. If your code states that all data must be reported truthfully, you do not even entertain the idea of hiding negative results from a client. You might lose short-term goodwill, but you preserve your integrity and keep a clean conscience.

Integrity is not about perfection. You will slip at times. The key is recognising your misstep, acknowledging it openly, and recalibrating to your principles. A code of honour is not an impossible standard. It is a steady commitment to do what is right, even when it is inconvenient or costly. By leading with integrity, you transform your presence into a living statement of reliability. In an era where loyalty is often fleeting, the leader who upholds a stable moral code becomes a beacon that others will want to rally around. That is the power of honour at work.

4. Strength with Compassion: Balancing Power and Kindness

Power can be intoxicating. Once you taste the authority to direct people's actions, it is tempting to become heavy-handed. Yet genuine leadership involves a more delicate balance: the fusion of strength with compassion. You must project authority firmly enough to guide your team yet remain approachable and empathetic enough that your people know you value their well-being. Lean too heavily into raw power, and you risk cultivating fear or resentment. Pivot too far into constant kindness, and you might lose the decisiveness needed to uphold standards. The sweet spot is found in integrating both qualities.

Think of Dr Martin Luther King Jr, known for leading the American civil rights movement in the mid-20th century. Although he had no formal political title, he wielded immense influence. He championed the rights of marginalised communities, refusing to accept injustice and organised mass protests that demanded radical reforms. Despite facing intimidation, harassment, and even imprisonment, he remained steadfast and strategic. Yet his strength never overshadowed his compassion. His speeches emphasised love, understanding, and empathy towards all people, including opponents. By combining moral authority with a gentle spirit, he inspired millions to stand behind him.

In your leadership journey, you might not face the same scale of struggle, but the principle endures. When your team falls behind schedule or commits serious errors, you have to be firm. Timelines must be met, and quality standards cannot be ignored. A leader who lacks firmness fosters chaos and mediocrity. You must communicate that deadlines are not optional and that repeated misconduct carries consequences. This shows respect for the organisation's goals and for those who are meeting standards diligently.

At the same time, compassion means recognising that people are not machines. They have families, mental health challenges, and personal aspirations. If you treat them purely as production units, you discard human dignity. A compassionate leader checks in with struggling team members, looking to understand the underlying reason for their performance dip. You might provide resources, adjust workloads, or grant them the support needed to recover. This does not undercut your authority. On the contrary, it strengthens trust. People see that you are not wielding power for its own sake; you are guiding the team toward mutual success.

Gallup polls over the years have consistently shown that employees who feel genuinely valued and supported by their leaders tend to surpass productivity goals by a significant margin. They are more likely to invest emotional energy in their tasks, solve problems collaboratively, and show loyalty during crises. The intangible connection fostered by empathy enhances overall engagement. This is where compassion becomes not just a moral choice but a strategic advantage.

Balancing power and kindness also influences how you address conflicts. If you tackle disputes solely by asserting your rank, you might force compliance but breed long-term resentment. A more enlightened method is to use your authority to maintain order while encouraging open dialogue about the real issues. You do not shy away from imposing rules or making final calls, but you also take time to listen to each person's stance. This approach respects the dignity of all involved. Over time, you create a culture where people feel safe speaking up, even if they disagree with you.

Another point to remember is how you carry yourself in casual settings. Leaders who appear unapproachable outside formal meetings might stifle relationships that could yield creative insights. A simple gesture like sharing a meal with your team or striking up genuine conversations in hallways can dismantle barriers. These moments give you a chance to display authentic kindness. People see that you are not merely a taskmaster but a human being who values connection.

However, do not mistake compassion for indefinite leniency. Holding others accountable remains essential. If someone repeatedly disrupts the team or refuses to grow, compassion might require you to let them go for the greater good. The difference lies in how you do it. You do not humiliate them or treat them with scorn. You communicate the decision clearly, treat them with respect, and part ways firmly but humanely. In doing so, you maintain the delicate equilibrium of strength and empathy that ensures your team's spirit remains intact.

Ultimately, the fusion of power and kindness defines a robust style of leadership that withstands the pressures of modern work environments. Your calm authority ensures that objectives are met, while your empathy ensures that your people remain energised, innovative, and loyal. This synergy allows you to lead with both the iron spine of conviction and the open heart of understanding. When individuals see that you hold them to a high standard but also value them as humans, you inspire a higher form of devotion and performance than raw force could ever achieve.

5. Fighting the Inner Enemy: Overcoming Doubt, Fear, and Ego

No enemy is more dangerous to a leader than the one within. External threats can be faced openly, but the silent saboteurs of doubt, fear, and ego gnaw at your resolve from the inside. They distort your judgement, undermine your confidence, and sow disharmony in your relationships. If you aim to walk the warrior's path, you must confront these internal adversaries with the same determination you would apply to any external foe.

Doubt often creeps in when you question your own capacity. It might whisper that you lack the experience to handle a new role or that others are more qualified. At first, doubt can appear constructive by urging you to prepare carefully, but unchecked, doubt becomes paralysing. One method to counter it is to gather evidence of your past achievements. Look at the moments when you overcame obstacles or earned respect by delivering results. Commit those wins to memory. Each time doubt arises, remind yourself that you have conquered challenges before and can do so again. This is not empty bragging; it is reaffirming proven truths to silence the unhelpful voice that says you are unworthy.

Fear is equally pervasive. It might revolve around failure, rejection, or loss of prestige. Some leaders respond by never taking risks, clinging to safe paths. This approach might shield them from criticism in the short run, yet it also blocks growth and innovation. One strategy to combat fear is to visualise the worst realistic outcome and plan how you would recover if it came to pass. This preparation removes the unknown element that magnifies fear. Once you realise you could navigate the downside, the phantoms lose their power. Another technique is to take incremental steps that desensitise you to fear. If you are terrified of public speaking, begin by presenting to smaller groups until your brain adjusts. Gradual exposure can reduce dread more effectively than avoidance.

Ego, on the other hand, deludes you with the illusion of invincibility. It tells you that your viewpoint is always correct, that you have surpassed the need for outside advice, or that your personal achievements overshadow the contributions of the team. Ego-driven leaders often alienate colleagues and stifle innovation because no one dares to question them. To keep your ego in check, surround yourself with a few trusted allies who will offer honest critique. If you find yourself brushing off their feedback, pause and ask why. Sometimes, your ego might be preventing you from accepting constructive insights. Remember that genuine strength is born from a willingness to learn, not from preening self-importance.

Studies from Imperial College London have highlighted the harmful impact of ego-driven leadership. Teams under leaders who frequently seek personal glory or shy away from collaborative processes show lower engagement and higher burnout rates. The research suggests that a leader's humility, including a readiness to admit errors and consult others, fosters a healthier, more creative work atmosphere. This underscores the principle that conquering your ego has tangible benefits for group success.

You must also develop ongoing self-reflection to keep these internal adversaries at bay. End each week by briefly reviewing where doubt, fear, or ego might have influenced your actions. Did you avoid a bold decision because you feared criticism. Did you dismiss a team member's suggestion because you assumed you knew better. Did you procrastinate on a crucial task because of underlying uncertainty about your capabilities. Being honest about these moments allows you to intercept destructive patterns before they harden into habits.

Another practical tool is seeking professional guidance, such as a mentor or leadership coach. A well-chosen mentor can spot the subtle signs of fear-driven avoidance or ego-driven rashness. They can also help you strategise ways to combat these tendencies. This does not mean outsourcing your self-development but supplementing it with an external perspective that accelerates your growth.

Finally, do not expect to conquer doubt, fear, and ego overnight. These inner enemies are tenacious. They will resurface at intervals, particularly when you step into new challenges. Instead of hoping to eliminate them permanently, aim to recognise their presence swiftly and thwart their influence. If you continually practise awareness, each round of confrontation becomes a learning experience that bolsters your resilience. Over time, you will be able to act in harmony with your values and lead with clarity, regardless of the internal chatter that tries to hold you back.

Conclusion

You have followed the warrior's path through trials, heartbreak, self-doubt, and all the storms that can threaten a leader's composure. You have examined why hardships are inevitable, discovered how mental toughness can insulate you from chaos, and reaffirmed the power of leading with a steadfast code of honour. You have also encountered the delicate balance of wielding strength with compassion, realising that true might is never cold or disconnected. Lastly, you have confronted the greatest challenge of all: the inner enemy of doubt, fear, and ego.

These principles are not abstract ideals. They are living disciplines you will apply daily as you navigate the demands of leadership. The warrior's path does not end once you have overcome a single crisis or achieved one moment of triumph. It continues through evolving challenges, each requiring renewed courage and an unwavering moral compass. By integrating what you have learned here, you can face ever-tougher trials and emerge with your honour, confidence, and sense of mission intact.

You now know that leadership is not about striding forward untested or unchallenged. It is about forging resilience in adversity, standing by your integrity when temptation lurks, and approaching your followers with empathy rather than sheer force. You have armed yourself with the mental, emotional, and ethical tools that define the warrior's path. Step forward with the knowledge that each challenge you meet can refine your calibre and amplify your influence. You are no longer merely a commander but a warrior-leader, poised to stand firm, serve others, and make choices worthy of your legacy.

CHAPTER 6

Leading In The Digital Age: Influence In A Changing World

You stand in a landscape transformed by technology. Information travels at lightning speed, and entire industries can rise or fall in the space of a single viral post. Authority is no longer confined to corner offices or formal titles. It is shaped, challenged, and reimagined every day on social media platforms and digital networks. If you aspire to be a leader in this dynamic terrain, you cannot rely on outdated strategies or the illusion that a strong personality alone will carry you. You must adapt, remain authentic, and harness the digital tools at your disposal without losing sight of timeless leadership values.

In this chapter, you will examine why chasing online popularity can undermine genuine leadership and how to build real influence in a world where attention spans are fleeting. You will see how the ongoing revolutions in AI, tech, and automation compel you to rethink decision-making, team structure, and the very nature of work. You will learn to manage crises in a hyperconnected environment, where news travels in seconds and misinformation can escalate swiftly. Finally, you will discover that despite the onslaught of digital trends, old-school leadership principles remain vital. The objective is not to reject modern tools but to use them with discernment and a commitment to your deeper mission. These insights will help you navigate a shifting world without sacrificing the integrity that makes you a leader worthy of respect.

1. The Social Media Trap: Leadership Beyond Likes and Follows

The sight of a skyrocketing follower count can tempt you to measure your leadership worth by online metrics. You may feel a surge of excitement when your posts get shared widely or when your face appears in the "trending" section. Yet, if you build your identity around digital applause, you risk neglecting what truly matters: creating tangible impact, fostering genuine relationships, and guiding your team through real-world obstacles. A leader who craves online fame can become preoccupied with surface-level recognition, forgetting that leadership demands substance beyond a highlight reel.

In the early days of Gymshark, founder Ben Francis leveraged social media influencers to promote his fledgling fitness clothing brand. The strategy helped fuel rapid growth, but Francis also understood that product quality, authentic customer engagement, and a committed culture behind the scenes would be the real foundation of long-term success. Had he relied solely on social media hype, Gymshark might have remained a transient phenomenon. Instead, Francis built a robust operation that stood even when certain influencers moved on. This illustrates the difference between using digital platforms as tools and letting them become your entire identity.

As a leader, you must keep a firm grip on your values while navigating social media currents. It is easy to chase trends for fleeting attention, only to discover that you have alienated core supporters or watered down your message. If you constantly pivot your organisation's direction to match whatever is "viral," you show a lack of consistency. Over time, people lose trust in leaders who shape-shift for the sake of popularity. Real authority emerges when you share thoughtful, relevant content that aligns with your mission, regardless of whether it wins universal applause.

Avoid the trap of vanity metrics such as likes, shares, or retweets. They can be helpful indicators of visibility, but they do not measure loyalty, respect, or the willingness of your audience to support your cause beyond a quick click. True engagement might take the form of deeper discussions, queries, or even constructive criticism. If you find that people are only praising you superficially or parroting slogans, you might have built a fan club rather than a community devoted to meaningful progress.

Responsible leaders also recognise the pitfalls of social media echo chambers. When you post, algorithms often funnel you into a group of like-minded individuals, reinforcing your existing views. This can create a false sense of consensus. When you step offline or talk to stakeholders outside your digital sphere, you might be stunned to find divergent opinions or mounting frustrations. Stepping outside your comfort zone by following voices that challenge your perspective can keep you grounded. This practice does not mean abandoning your principles, but it helps you remain aware of realities that do not trend in your curated feed.

Moreover, a reliance on social media can erode the personal touch that sustains robust leadership. Dashing off posts or quick replies might be efficient, but it rarely equals the depth of face-to-face interaction or well-considered dialogue. If you want to forge trust in your team, schedule genuine conversations, video chats, or personal check-ins. Encourage employees to communicate concerns privately rather than airing them in open digital forums where misunderstandings can escalate. Real human contact fosters bonds that cyberspace alone cannot replicate.

Ultimately, social media is neither an enemy nor a saviour. It is a tool that can magnify your message or distort your identity, depending on how you wield it. By remaining grounded in genuine values and refusing to chase superficial applause, you break free from the trap of equating leadership with online status. Instead, you present your authentic self, engage with supporters meaningfully, and use technology to amplify a mission that can thrive in the real world, not just on a screen.

2. Building Real Influence in a World of Short Attention Spans

You live in a constant barrage of notifications, pop-up ads, and endless scrolling. The average individual flicks through multiple pieces of content every few seconds, evaluating whether something is worth more than a glance. In such a landscape, you might believe that reducing everything to bite-sized slogans is the only way to hold attention. Yet genuine influence seldom springs from watered-down messages. If you want to shape opinions and drive actual change, you must learn to convey depth in a concise yet captivating way.

Bear Grylls, known for survival television programmes, has excelled at engaging audiences with impactful messages in short segments. His format entertains viewers with high-adrenaline scenarios, but he also embeds practical life lessons. He demonstrates resilience, adaptation, and mental toughness in episodes rarely longer than an hour. Although he operates within a medium where viewers can switch channels instantly, Bear's ability to share both excitement and knowledge keeps his audience enthralled. He has proved that you can communicate meaningful ideas in a world that seems addicted to quick consumption.

To build genuine influence, start by clarifying what you stand for. A scattergun approach may gather fleeting interest but will not hold your audience's loyalty. Identify the core messages you want to share, the values you refuse to compromise, and the specific ways you intend to uplift those around you. A crisp, well-defined purpose stands out amid the digital noise because it offers substance people can latch onto. If someone sees you consistently champion a clear principle, they know you are not merely chasing the latest fad.

Next, find methods to package depth into digestible formats. This does not mean dumbing down your content. Rather, it means structuring it so that each point feels like a stepping stone leading to a more significant concept. For instance, if you want to teach a complex leadership principle, break it into a short introduction, a brief example, and a concise takeaway. If you are speaking publicly, use storytelling to illustrate your argument. Humans are wired to pay attention to narratives, so weaving a brief anecdote into your explanation can keep eyes on you longer than a dry list of bullet points.

Another strategy is to engage actively rather than broadcasting. If your leadership presence is purely one-way, where you talk and everyone else listens, you risk losing your audience to more interactive experiences. Set up question-and-answer segments, encourage discussions, and invite followers or team members to contribute their viewpoints. When people feel like participants rather than passive spectators, they pay closer attention. They also develop a sense of investment that extends your influence beyond the moment.

Adapt your communication style based on context. What works in a fast-paced social media environment might differ from what resonates in an internal meeting or a keynote speech. Keep a finger on the pulse of your audience's preferences and adjust your format accordingly. Some leaders host regular live sessions where they tackle a single crucial topic at length, offering room for deeper understanding. Others create short, sharp pieces of content for daily insights while reserving lengthier discussions for private forums or workshops. By tailoring your approach, you increase the odds of capturing and retaining attention.

Finally, recognise that short attention spans do not equate to shallow intelligence. Many individuals crave thought-provoking content but are simply inundated by competing messages. If you deliver something both meaningful and packaged efficiently, you can cut through the clutter. The key is consistency. Show up regularly, deliver genuine insights, and remain authentic. Over time, your audience will realise you offer something of value rather than quick thrills. This fosters trust and ensures that when you speak, people stop scrolling and start listening.

By refining your ability to engage short attention spans with real depth, you unlock a new dimension of leadership influence. You prove that complex ideas, moral clarity, and tangible guidance can fit into a fast-moving world. More than ever, people hunger for authenticity beneath the surface-level hype. If you remain focused, prepared, and determined to share real substance, you will resonate in places where superficial content fades as swiftly as it appears.

3. The Digital Revolution: How AI, Tech, and Automation Impact Leadership

Leading In The Digital Age: Influence In A Changing World

The age of digital disruption is not coming; it is already here. Rapid developments in artificial intelligence, cloud computing, and robotic automation have reshaped industries from manufacturing to finance. As a leader, you cannot afford to treat technology as a minor addition to your strategy. Instead, you must face a reality where digital tools transform your workforce, redefine skill sets, and create new ethical dilemmas. The manner in which you adapt will determine whether you guide your team to fresh opportunities or watch as they drift toward irrelevance.

When Satya Nadella took over as CEO of Microsoft in 2014, he steered the company away from an insular culture and into a cloud-centric enterprise ready to compete in a rapidly evolving market. By embracing new technology and shifting towards software-as-a-service, Nadella spurred growth and repositioned Microsoft as a key player in cloud solutions. His leadership displayed two essential qualities for thriving amid digital change: a willingness to learn and the ability to pivot core strategies. Stagnation in this environment is no longer an option.

For you, the first step in mastering the digital revolution is to remain curious. Regularly exploring new developments in AI or data analytics is not a chore but a necessity. You do not need to become a software engineer, but you should grasp the practical implications of emerging tools. If your job involves leading a product team, you might investigate how machine learning can reduce repetitive tasks, improve user experience, or offer predictive insights. If you run a sales division, you might examine how analytics can identify hidden trends in customer behaviour. Curiosity keeps you agile, ready to adopt novel approaches when they can elevate your organisation.

You also need to refine the skills that machines cannot duplicate, at least not yet. Creativity, empathy, and complex problem-solving remain human strengths that are not easily replaced by algorithms. Encourage your team to hone these attributes through collaboration and continuous learning. If routine tasks are automated, invest the freed-up time into more strategic or creative pursuits. The leaders who excel in this era will be those who recognise that technology can liberate human potential for roles that require insight, diplomacy, and moral judgement.

Ethical leadership becomes paramount in a digital world. Algorithms can reflect biases lurking in historical data, leading to unjust outcomes if not monitored carefully. Automation can displace workers if you implement it without a plan for retraining or redeploying talent. Address these dilemmas proactively. Set up committees or working groups to spot potential ethical pitfalls before they escalate. Collaborate with IT experts who can help build transparency and accountability into your organisation's use of AI. By doing so, you maintain public trust and safeguard your team's morale.

Another challenge is managing virtual or hybrid teams. You might find yourself leading groups scattered across different time zones who rarely meet in person. Communication becomes more complex, as you must adapt to video calls, digital collaboration tools, and asynchronous workflows. In this scenario, clarity is your ally. Make objectives, deadlines, and processes explicit so that no one is left guessing. Foster relationships by scheduling informal check-ins, encouraging online social gatherings, or using chat platforms that keep the human connection alive. A leader who masters virtual engagement can galvanise diverse teams far more efficiently than one relying solely on face-to-face interaction.

Finally, expect the pace of change to accelerate. New technologies can explode onto the scene and disrupt your carefully laid plans in months or even weeks. This means you cannot rely on a single, unchanging strategic blueprint. Instead, cultivate a culture of experimentation and feedback loops. Small pilot projects let you test new tools without risking your entire operation. If they thrive, scale up quickly. If they fail, learn from the misstep and move on. This cyclical process of testing, learning, and adapting is the hallmark of a digitally savvy leader.

In essence, the digital revolution demands both openness to novelty and an unyielding commitment to human values. By staying curious, nurturing the human side of leadership, and tackling ethical questions head-on, you ensure that technology elevates your mission rather than derails it. In doing so, you prove that digital progress and timeless leadership principles need not clash; they can strengthen one another as you steer your team into a new frontier.

4. Crisis Management in a Hyperconnected World

In an era when a single social media post can spark uproar across continents, crises no longer unfold slowly behind closed doors. They detonate in public view, where the world watches and reacts in real time. A small misstep or overlooked detail can balloon into global headlines overnight, catching you off guard unless you are equipped to respond effectively. Leadership under these conditions demands speed, transparency, and the ability to maintain composure when the pressure mounts.

Brian Chesky, co-founder of Airbnb, faced a severe test when the pandemic crushed the travel and hospitality sector. Bookings plummeted, revenue declined sharply, and the company had to let go of a large portion of its staff. Rather than hide behind closed doors, Chesky issued a public letter explaining the rationale, the steps taken to support departing employees, and the long-term vision for recovery. His clear communication and empathetic tone earned respect from staff, investors, and customers at a time when cynicism ran high. This example underlines a core truth: Leadership in crisis is not about spin or denial but addressing problems head-on and showing a sense of responsibility that others can rally around.

You must act swiftly but not impulsively. In a hyperconnected environment, time is of the essence. If you delay acknowledging an issue, whether it is a data breach, a product failure, or a public relations mishap, the narrative can spiral out of your control. Take immediate steps to gather the facts, verify them, and prepare a concise statement. Even if you do not have all the answers yet, letting people know you are investigating the matter shows seriousness. Misinformation flourishes in a vacuum of official communication, so beat the rumours by stating what you can confirm, followed by what you intend to find out next.

Transparency is the backbone of crisis management. If you attempt to mask a scandal or minimise damage by distorting the truth, the digital world's collective gaze will likely uncover inconsistencies. Once your credibility is tarnished, it can be an uphill battle to regain trust. Leaders who meet crises with honesty, even when revealing uncomfortable details, often find that stakeholders appreciate openness. Naturally, you must exercise discretion about confidential data or legal constraints, but you can do so while still being as forthright as circumstances allow.

Empathy plays a decisive role, too. People affected by the crisis- employees, customers, or partners- want to see that you understand their concerns and plan to address them. This means avoiding cold corporate phrases or vague statements that sidestep responsibility. A heartfelt admission of mistakes, coupled with a plan to rectify them, can soothe anger and limit backlash. Even if you are not personally at fault, taking ownership of the path forward demonstrates the brand of leadership people respect.

Rapid decision-making also becomes essential. In a hyperconnected crisis, developments happen almost by the minute. You might need to halt a problematic product line, launch a new customer service channel, or issue refunds on a large scale. Indecision or prolonged debates can worsen the situation as frustration and anger grow among those expecting swift action. Setting up a dedicated crisis response team with clear authority to act can accelerate resolutions. This unit gathers the latest information, evaluates options, and executes promptly.

After stabilising the immediate threats, your final move involves rebuilding trust and learning lessons. Conduct a thorough post-mortem to identify root causes, whether they lie in oversight, miscommunication, or flawed processes. Implement changes to prevent a recurrence and communicate these adjustments openly. By doing so, you turn a crisis into a catalyst for progress, showing that your organisation is not only reactive but determined to grow stronger.

Leading in a hyperconnected world leaves no room for complacency. You must stay vigilant, prepared, and ready to communicate at a moment's notice. Crises will happen, but they need not spell doom for your leadership. With calm honesty, swift action, and a willingness to accept responsibility, you can emerge from turmoil with your credibility intact. More than that, you can gain the respect of onlookers who see that, under the glare of digital scrutiny, you uphold the standards of honourable leadership and pave the way for a more resilient future.

5. The Return to Authenticity: Why Old-School Leadership Still Wins

In a world bombarded by digital transformations, you might assume traditional leadership principles have expired. Yet the truth is that old-school virtues, straight talking, consistency, and face-to-face rapport, remain as vital as ever. Technology can amplify your voice, but it cannot replicate the depth of personal connections forged through sincerity and reliability. You will find that in times of uncertainty, people gravitate towards leaders who exhibit grounded, time-honoured qualities.

Michael O'Leary, the longtime chief executive of Ryanair, is known for a brash and occasionally controversial style. While many disagree with his approach, he has retained a core authenticity that resonates with his airline's budget-focused ethos. He speaks bluntly about fares, keeps operations streamlined, and shows no interest in pandering to shifting public sentiments. Despite creating waves in media, O'Leary's straightforward manner has secured a loyal customer base that appreciates the airline's clear-cut promise: low prices and minimal frills. His example highlights that authenticity, however direct or unpolished, can earn trust even in a competitive market.

If you want to wield this old-school authenticity, begin by speaking plainly. In an age of corporate jargon and sugar-coated statements, candour stands out. When you communicate tasks, goals, or challenges, avoid buzzwords that dilute meaning. Let your team or audience know exactly what needs to be done, why it is crucial, and how everyone can contribute. This directness fosters an atmosphere where confusion has little room to take root. People appreciate leaders who do not waste their time or hide realities behind polished language.

Consistency is another hallmark of the timeless leader. If you change course every week, chasing trends or reacting to social media uproar, your team will grow weary. Standing by your core principles while adapting tactics as needed assures people that you are not merely influenced by fleeting whims. This does not imply rigidity. Instead, it signals that you have a solid moral and strategic foundation, and that changes you introduce are purposeful, not haphazard.

Face-to-face interaction remains powerful, even in a society that thrives on digital connectivity. Whenever possible, invest time in personal meetings, site visits, or genuine video calls where you actually engage rather than multitask. Shake hands, observe body language, and gauge real-time reactions. Technology is helpful, but it can create artificial barriers. A sincere conversation, where you look someone in the eye, has a different weight than an email or a quick text. People remember leaders who take the time to be present in person, especially in crucial moments such as conflict resolution, performance reviews, or significant announcements.

This pursuit of authenticity also involves self-awareness. You cannot be genuine if you are unsure of who you are or what you stand for. Reflect on your leadership style, your strengths, and your blind spots. If you are prone to blunt speech like O'Leary, be mindful of when it might harm sensitive negotiations. If you are more soft-spoken, ensure your gentleness does not translate into passivity when firm decisions are required. Know yourself, and then show up consistently rather than pretending to be a different person for the sake of public perception.

Lastly, be prepared to accept that authenticity will not please everyone. Some might criticise your refusal to adapt to every trend or your direct style of communication. However, the loyalty you build among those who appreciate your clarity outweighs the disapproval of those seeking something else. Over time, many come to respect a leader who remains genuine in a world full of shifting facades. This kind of respect leads to a stable foundation of trust that can endure digital disruptions and changing economic conditions.

Old-school leadership thrives because it speaks to human fundamentals. People want honesty, reliability, and a sense that their leader is not merely following headlines but living by convictions. No app or digital platform can replace that ethos. By marrying time-honoured attributes with modern tools, you create a leadership style that feels solid and innovative simultaneously, giving your team the best of both worlds. In a fast-paced era, that combination is a beacon of reassurance, proving that no matter how the world evolves, integrity and authenticity remain unshakable.

Conclusion

Leading In The Digital Age: Influence In A Changing World

You have explored the shifting currents of digital influence and discovered that while new technology changes the rules of engagement, the core of leadership endures. Social media can either elevate your message or trap you in a shallow quest for likes. Short attention spans demand concise impact, yet substance still reigns when properly delivered. AI and automation present limitless opportunities, but they also test your ethical boundaries and highlight the need for distinctly human qualities like empathy and creativity. Hyperconnected crises erupt faster than ever, demanding swift, transparent responses that reinforce trust. And despite all these transformations, old-school authenticity, rooted in clarity, reliability, and direct human connection, remains a timeless anchor in your leadership toolkit.

As you move forward, do not treat technology as a magic wand or a menace. See it as a resource that amplifies whatever leadership qualities you choose to embody. Stay current with digital trends, but never trade your integrity for fleeting online approval. Evolve your communication style to match fast-paced contexts, yet ensure it does not erode depth or empathy. Keep an eye on emerging innovations, but remember that it is your moral compass and emotional intelligence that will ultimately steer you and your team through a rapidly changing world.

Leaders who thrive in the digital age combine agility and principle. They use tools that enhance productivity and outreach without letting the medium overshadow the message. They build global networks while valuing old-fashioned virtues like sincerity and fair dealing. In this delicate balance lies the future of leadership: adaptive, humane, and unwavering in its ethical stance. If you continue to walk this path, you will find that the world of tomorrow, no matter how high-tech, will always have space for leaders who stand resolute in purpose and unshakeable in character.

CHAPTER 7

Leading Through Crisis: What To Do When Everything Falls Apart

You will face moments when the world around you crumbles. Financial meltdowns, public scandals, or unforeseen disasters can arise with devastating force. In these moments, your title alone will not save you. Your carefully planned strategies may collapse overnight. What remains is your ability to adapt, calm the storm, and guide others through the wreckage. This chapter focuses on how to lead when everything seems to be falling apart.

You will explore how exceptional leaders steady themselves in the eye of the storm and project confidence under immense pressure. You will discover why fear grips people so easily and how you can channel that energy toward unity rather than chaos. You will learn techniques for making decisions amid deafening noise, ensuring you filter out distractions to maintain a rational course. You will see how taking responsibility, even for failures that are not entirely your fault, can preserve credibility when every eye turns to you for answers.

Finally, you will find ways to restore trust after a leadership mistake has shaken people's confidence. By the end of this chapter, you will be equipped with the mindset, the action steps, and the moral conviction to lead in the darkest of times. You will stand as the calm centre when the world spins out of control, prepared to keep your team focused, hopeful, and ready to fight another day.

1. The Calm in the Storm: How Great Leaders Handle Crisis

When disaster strikes, your team will look to you for signals on how to react. If you freeze or display panic, you give them permission to unravel. If you project steady composure, you inspire them to steady themselves as well. A crisis reveals character. It shows whether your leadership values are mere words or deeply held principles that guide your conduct under strain. The ability to remain calm in a storm stems from mental preparation, practical drills, and an unwavering belief that you can find a way forward even if the situation looks dire.

One real-world illustration comes from Captain Tammie Jo Shults, an airline pilot who made headlines when she safely landed a damaged passenger jet in 2018. A catastrophic engine failure led to chaos on board. Despite the mayhem, Captain Shults maintained a calm, measured tone. She communicated clearly with air traffic control and her crew, indicating precisely what she needed and what was happening. That composure under extreme circumstances reassured terrified passengers and allowed her to execute a safe landing. In interviews afterward, she credited repetitive flight simulations and mental rehearsals for enabling her to react without panic. Through discipline and pre-emptive training, her calm demeanour became a natural reflex rather than a forced act.

In a corporate context, crisis drills serve a similar purpose. Companies in high-risk sectors, such as cybersecurity or energy, often run simulated catastrophes to gauge how quickly employees can respond. You might organise a weekend exercise where your team faces a hypothetical scenario: a massive data breach, a sudden supply chain failure, or an urgent recall of faulty products. By testing responses in a controlled environment, you teach everyone to prioritise the right actions over emotional reactions. In times of real turmoil, that muscle memory kicks in, reducing the likelihood of chaos overwhelming rational thought.

Calm leadership also requires clear communication. Within minutes of a crisis, rumours can spread. Fragmented information leads to speculation, which breeds panic. Your role is to stand above the confusion and relay accurate updates. Even if you do not have all the facts yet, acknowledging what you do know and stating what you plan to find out builds credibility. People can cope with honest uncertainty but not with glaring silence. Provide regular briefings, outline next steps, and designate a point of contact for questions. A structured flow of information becomes a lifeline when nerves are frayed.

Another vital piece is emotional control. Anxiety levels surge when unforeseen disasters strike. Your own adrenaline will surge, too. The trick is not to pretend you feel nothing but to master your emotional response so that it does not paralyse your decision-making. Simple grounding techniques, like controlled breathing or a moment of silent focus before speaking, can diffuse panic. If your team sees you keeping your composure, they will be more inclined to mirror that state of mind. The result is a calmer group dynamic and an environment more conducive to finding viable solutions.

You should also create a command structure that clarifies roles. In the heat of a crisis, your direct involvement in every detail might be impossible. Therefore, identify key individuals who can handle separate tasks, whether that is coordinating with emergency services, communicating with the press, or overseeing internal operations. By delegating effectively, you prevent a single point of failure. People know exactly where to go for instructions, ensuring quick responses rather than frantic guesswork.

Finally, demonstrate empathy. People's fears are real and can intensify if they feel neglected. Taking a few moments to acknowledge the gravity of a crisis can help. Show that you understand the emotional toll, then guide them towards constructive action. This balance, recognising human vulnerability while maintaining focus, earns loyalty and steadies collective morale. Calm in the storm is not about detaching from reality; it is about confronting harsh truths with measured resolve.

When you cultivate these habits, mental rehearsals, disciplined communication, role clarity, and empathy, you transform your presence into a stabilising force. Others will look to you for strength, and you will provide it by acting, not panicking. A crisis can make or break a leader's reputation. Stand calm in the heart of chaos, and you will not only survive but emerge with greater respect from those who followed your lead under pressure.

2. The Psychology of Panic: Leading Others When Fear Takes Over

Crises often trigger a wave of panic that spreads through a team like wildfire. Fear is contagious. Once the first few voices start to tremble, the rest can quickly follow unless you step in to guide emotions in a more productive direction. To do this, you need a basic understanding of why panic arises and how you can redirect it.

An illustrative case is what happened at a large finance firm in Hong Kong during the 1998 Asian financial crisis. The sudden collapse of regional currencies and markets ignited widespread anxiety. Rumours of layoffs and bankruptcy circulated, leading some employees to pre-emptively clear their desks and walk out. In response, a department leader gathered her team in a conference room and offered a straightforward briefing on the company's current standing. She acknowledged the severity of the situation without minimising it, but she also shared the specific steps senior management was taking to secure liquidity. By offering a balanced view, honest about the risk yet also focused on the tangible actions in motion, she managed to halt the exodus. Most staff members decided to stay, calmer now that they had clear information. This episode highlights the power of proactive reassurance in quelling panic before it dominates.

Why does panic take hold so swiftly? Neuroscientists point to the amygdala, the part of the brain that processes threats. In uncertain times, this fight-or-flight response can override logical thinking. People become hypersensitive to cues of danger, and they grasp at any rumour or sign that might confirm their worst fears. Leaders who understand this biological mechanism can intervene with well-timed, transparent messaging. When your team realises you have a rational plan, or at least a method to create one, the amygdala is less likely to hijack their minds.

Rapid communication is your best defence. If your organisation faces an external crisis, do not wait days to address it. A delay fuels speculation. Instead, hold a short briefing or send an immediate group message acknowledging the situation, stating any confirmed facts, and giving a sense of the timeline for updates. This way, your team has a reference point to counter alarming gossip. When false narratives arise, they can refer to your statement and see if new information matches it. This straightforward step can block panic from metastasising.

You can also use the technique of reframing. Fear of the unknown amplifies anxiety. But if you reshape that fear as a challenge, something the group can tackle with collective strength, you divert panic into problem-solving. For instance, you might say, "Yes, this situation is unprecedented, but we have tackled similar hurdles before. Let's list the resources we still have, find creative angles, and work out a contingency plan together." By naming specific tasks, you replace swirling dread with a tangible sense of purpose. That shift from helplessness to action often interrupts panic and inspires a determined outlook.

Empathy is equally vital. Telling panicked individuals to "calm down" rarely helps. Instead, acknowledge their fears. You might say, "I understand why you feel alarmed. This is unsettling for all of us." Once they feel validated, they are more open to hearing rational proposals. Dismissing or ridiculing fear only deepens the sense of isolation and helplessness. Show compassion first, then guide the conversation toward constructive steps.

Lastly, identify panic "hotspots" within your team, those few employees who tend to escalate tension. Pull them aside for a private discussion if needed. Often, they are not trying to cause trouble but lack the tools to manage their stress. Giving them extra clarity or responsibilities that channel their nervous energy productively can make them allies rather than alarmists. In some cases, you may have to be firm if someone persists in spreading false rumours, but an empathetic approach should be your starting point.

By understanding the psychology of panic, you gain an advantage in crisis management. You know how to step between raw fear and a stable atmosphere. Rather than letting panic paralyse your team, you transform anxiety into a shared resolve. In times of crisis, that leadership skill can mean the difference between organisational collapse and a disciplined effort that finds a way through the darkest hours.

3. Decision-Making in Chaos: Separating Noise from What Matters

When a crisis rages, information floods in from every angle. You might receive frantic emails, contradicting data, and urgent demands from multiple stakeholders. The volume can be overwhelming. In this chaos, effective decisions hinge on your ability to sift out the irrelevant noise and focus on what truly impacts outcomes. Doing so requires a systematic approach, self-discipline, and the courage to act once you have enough information, knowing you will never possess a perfect set of facts.

A notable example emerges from the 2010 Chilean mining accident, where 33 miners were trapped underground for 69 days. The rescue effort attracted intense global attention. Chilean officials had to coordinate with engineers, drilling experts, health professionals, and even NASA consultants. Media outlets worldwide clamoured for updates. Politicians weighed in. With so many voices offering strategies, it would have been easy to drown in proposals. Yet the leadership team on site concentrated on a few central data points: the miners' physical location, the geological structure around them, the technical feasibility of each rescue drill, and the timelines associated with each approach. By filtering out extraneous detail, such as political squabbling, they maintained a clear path that ultimately led to a successful rescue. Their priority was straightforward: sustain the miners' well-being and secure a safe extraction. That clarity protected them from being engulfed by the sheer volume of outside input.

For you, the first step is to define the core question at hand. In a business crisis, is your immediate priority to stabilise cash flow, protect customer relationships, or address a public relations nightmare? Each emergency might have a different focal point, but identify it without delay. If you try to solve everything at once, you solve nothing. Once you set a dominant objective, you can rank incoming data by how directly it relates to that objective. If a piece of information does not affect your core target, you can put it aside for later review.

Data triage is your next line of defence. As you receive new details, sort them quickly into categories: critical, useful, irrelevant. If something is critical, it affects your ability to achieve your main goal right now. Useful data might provide background insight but does not require immediate attention. Irrelevant items may be speculation or tangential aspects that can wait. Keep a running document, digital or on paper, where you track your main objective, your known facts, and the key uncertainties. Updating this list regularly keeps your mind uncluttered. You avoid the trap of re-checking emails or messages for the same points over and over.

Consulting a small, trusted group can also sharpen your decision-making. Choose individuals with direct expertise rather than a broad committee that might add more noise. A finance specialist can confirm which expenses must be prioritised. A technical expert can clarify what is truly feasible under crisis conditions. This streamlined approach ensures you gather relevant counsel while preventing endless debate.

Make it clear that once you have heard their inputs, you will decide on the course of action. Extend genuine thanks for their perspectives, but remember the final responsibility is yours.

Timing matters enormously. In chaos, delays can create a vacuum where rumours fester. That does not mean you rush blindly, but you recognise when you have reached the point of diminishing returns on further data gathering. There is a moment when seeking additional facts no longer reduces uncertainty, it only postpones action. The best leaders trust their judgment once they have a critical mass of the right information and they move forward decisively. If new events unfold, they adjust as needed, but they do not remain stuck in indecision.

You must also accept that not all your calls will be perfect. In crisis mode, mistakes are inevitable. The key is to pivot fast. If you find your choice was flawed, communicate it openly, shift direction, and maintain momentum. This willingness to adapt under pressure, rather than doubling down on a failing path, preserves your credibility.

Above all, never lose sight of your guiding values in the scramble for quick fixes. Compromising ethical standards or disrespecting your team's well-being for a short-term patch often leads to deeper problems later. Even in chaos, let your moral compass steer you. By coupling that integrity with disciplined data triage and decisive action, you can cut through the noise and direct your team with clarity and purpose.

4. The Power of Ownership: Taking Responsibility for Failures

In the midst of a crisis, you may feel a powerful temptation to shift blame or distance yourself from what has gone wrong. Yet the quickest way to lose trust is to point fingers when things unravel. True leadership demands ownership. Even if external forces triggered the trouble, you stand at the helm. You are accountable for the way your organisation responds. Owning that responsibility might feel like a burden, but it is also a potent force that can unite a fractured team behind a shared purpose.

A striking illustration comes from Gerald Ratner, the British businessman behind Ratners Jewellers, who faced a now-famous debacle in the early 1990s. During a speaking engagement, Ratner made disparaging remarks about his own products, calling them "total rubbish." The backlash was swift and brutal; the firm's value plummeted. Ratner initially tried to explain his remarks as light-hearted banter gone wrong, but the public remained unconvinced. Eventually, he had to confront the damage head-on. He accepted fault and worked to repair the brand's reputation, though the struggle was immense. The lesson is clear: the moment you try to deflect responsibility in a crisis, you only widen the gap between yourself and those you lead.

When you demonstrate ownership, you show that your ego is not the priority. You acknowledge the team's disappointment and outline what will be done to fix the situation. You might say, "I authorised this plan, and it has caused serious setbacks. I take full responsibility. Here are the steps we will take to rectify it." Such honesty does not make you appear weak. On the contrary, it displays courage and sincerity. Your team or stakeholders may be angry, but they are more likely to stand with you if they see you owning the misstep rather than dodging it.

Owning a failure also gives you the moral standing to challenge your team to do better. If you refuse to admit your share of the blame, you lose any legitimacy when asking them to accept their own roles in the crisis. By stepping forward, you break the cycle of blame and focus everyone's attention on solutions. You encourage a culture where people can acknowledge mistakes quickly, which speeds up learning. Such openness, while risky in the short term, creates long-term resilience.

You must also move swiftly from ownership to rectification. Words alone will not solve the crisis. Draft a plan that details how you will address the immediate harm, whether that is financial losses, reputational damage, or operational breakdowns. Assign clear responsibilities for executing each part of the recovery strategy. If the fault lies partly in your own decisions, detail how you will avoid repeating the same errors. For instance, you might revise quality control processes, implement new checks and balances, or rotate responsibilities so that one person is never left in sole control of a critical area.

It is worth noting that sometimes, you will be the scapegoat for issues well beyond your control. Taking ownership does not mean you claim you personally caused every failing. It means you refuse to hide behind excuses. You stand as the accountable figure who will lead the charge to fix the damage. This approach often transforms even the most hostile environments into a place where your team sees hope. They realise that, despite the chaos, someone is steering the ship with a steady hand.

By embracing responsibility, you also help your team maintain morale. People often feel powerless in a crisis, especially if they cannot pinpoint what went wrong. Seeing you acknowledge the problem and commit to solutions gives them a sense of direction. They understand where the lines of accountability run and can focus on collective repair rather than fruitless blame-shifting.

Finally, ownership paves the way for rebuilding trust. If those you lead see you handle adversity with candour, they are likelier to believe you truly have the team's interests at heart. It fosters loyalty that mere success could never buy. Anyone can stand tall in victory, but only the genuine leader remains upright and forthright in defeat. Your willingness to shoulder responsibility can turn a catastrophic failure into a catalyst for deeper unity and renewed determination across your entire organisation.

5. How to Rebuild Trust After a Leadership Mistake

Even the strongest leaders slip. Perhaps you misjudged a situation, overlooked critical warnings, or made a rash decision that led to a major setback. Once the dust settles, you will need to mend the damage. Trust, once fractured, does not heal automatically. It requires a diligent, transparent process that shows you have learnt your lesson and that you value the people you lead more than your personal pride.

A well-known example is the shift undertaken by Nokia when its management acknowledged failing to keep pace with smartphone innovations in the late 2000s. After losing significant market share, the company leadership had to face both staff and global partners who felt let down. Rather than concealing the scale of the collapse, the new leadership team outlined a restructuring plan, openly admitting past miscalculations. They engaged employees at all levels, asking them to suggest solutions and new directions. Although Nokia never reclaimed its former dominance, it gradually rebuilt credibility in the telecoms sector, eventually pivoting towards infrastructure and licensing. The move demonstrates how candid acknowledgement and collaborative, forward planning can rebuild a measure of trust even after a damaging leadership oversight.

Step one is to openly apologise without drowning in self-justification. A sincere apology acknowledges the real consequences of your actions. Rather than saying, "I'm sorry you felt upset," which shifts blame to others' feelings, a better approach is ", I'm sorry for my decision that caused this negative outcome." Such phrasing accepts responsibility. It respects the experiences of those who were affected, and it sets the tone for genuine remorse.

Next, you must provide a roadmap for how things will improve. People are hesitant to trust again if they think you are likely to repeat the same mistake. Detail the specific changes you are making, whether that is introducing new risk assessments, seeking external audits, or revising internal processes. Show that you have learnt not just from the immediate error but from the broader circumstances that allowed it to happen. This level of introspection signals you are not sweeping the incident under the rug.

Involve those who lost trust in the rebuilding effort. Ask for their insights, incorporate their feedback into your new strategies, and demonstrate that you value their perspective. That might require uncomfortable conversations, especially if emotions are still running high. However, inviting them into the solution affirms that you respect them as partners rather than mere bystanders. When they see their suggestions shaping policy or practice, they begin to believe in your new commitment.

Transparency is paramount during this stage. Regularly update your team on the progress of your remedial measures. If you announced a major overhaul in how customer complaints are handled, provide weekly or monthly reports on improvements. If you promised more rigorous safety standards, share tangible milestones as they are achieved. The more you shine a light on each step forward, the more people will see that your words are not empty. This clarity helps rebuild the emotional bank account of trust that got drained by your mistake.

Patience is also key. Trust is like a fragile vase. Once cracked, it can be repaired, but the process is delicate. You cannot force people to trust you again overnight. Accept that some individuals may remain cautious for a while. Focus on consistent, dependable behaviour rather than grand gestures. If you deliver on every promise you make from this point onward, you gradually restore confidence. Over time, even the most hurt stakeholders may come around if they see unwavering sincerity in your efforts.

Lastly, reflect on the personal growth this process can bring. A leadership mistake is painful, but it is also an opportunity for deeper self-awareness. Use this chance to refine your decision-making style, your communication approach, and your relationship with your team. In many cases, leaders who navigate a major mistake with honesty and constructive action end up forging even stronger bonds. The adversity becomes a shared chapter of transformation. Through openness, accountability, and consistent improvement, you can emerge from the shadow of error with renewed respect and a fortified sense of unity across your organisation.

Conclusion

Leading through crisis lays bare your fundamental qualities. The chaos tests your resolve, your emotional intelligence, and your ethical backbone. By maintaining a calm poise, you anchor those around you when panic might otherwise take over. By understanding the deep-rooted psychology of fear, you can direct your team's energies toward positive action. You filter through the noise to find essential facts, enabling you to make quick but informed choices. You hold yourself responsible for failures, securing the moral authority to guide the rebuilding process. And when your own mistakes shatter trust, you learn to restore it through honest engagement, transparent strategies, and unwavering dedication to improvement.

Every leader hopes crises will be rare, but reality often has other plans. Whether the breakdown arises from economic turbulence, a product defect, or a sudden scandal, you will need these tools to steer your team to safer ground. You have now gathered insights on balancing composure with empathy, decisive action with humility, and immediate urgency with long-term lessons. Carry these principles as an integral part of your leadership arsenal. When calamity strikes, you will not merely endure. You will lead, offering the kind of stability and direction that turns disaster into a chapter of renewal rather than defeat.

CHAPTER 8

The Legacy Of A Leader: Mentorship And Impact

You have navigated harsh tests, guided teams under pressure, and honed your code of conduct. By now, you understand that leadership is about more than hitting targets or enjoying titles. A truly great leader leaves a lasting impression that continues to shape others long after you step away. You do not seek a quick round of applause but a transformation that endures across generations. This is where legacy comes into play.

In this chapter, you will explore how your ultimate mark as a leader rests not in commanding followers but in raising new leaders. You will discover that mentorship is more than an informal chat; it is a structured yet personal mission to prepare others for the front lines of responsibility. You will see why putting others before yourself is a mark of the strongest leadership and how such selflessness ripples far beyond your immediate circle. You will learn how to create a legacy that stands the test of time, and you will face the difficult art of stepping away with honour once your mission is done. Through these insights, you will gain a perspective on leadership that transcends day-to-day victories. Your legacy becomes the sum of all the lives you shape and the future you empower them to create.

1. Why Great Leaders Don't Create Followers, They Create More Leaders

The Legacy Of A Leader: Mentorship And Impact

You might have heard the old phrase, "A boss wants subordinates; a leader wants more leaders." This distinction is crucial for anyone who aims to leave a mark that endures beyond a single project or era. True leadership is not about gathering cheerleaders who simply applaud your every move. It is about forging a cadre of individuals who can one day guide teams, innovate, and make decisions with the same integrity and drive that you uphold. A leader of this calibre sees beyond personal ambition and invests in growing the leadership capacity of others.

One striking example is Bill Campbell, an influential mentor in Silicon Valley who advised the founders of Google, Apple, and many rising startups. Campbell's approach was not about maintaining a fan club. Instead, he spent time nurturing each executive's strategic thinking, emotional intelligence, and resilience under stress. He acted as a coach who saw his true accomplishment in how many new trailblazers he helped unleash into the tech world. By the end of his life, he had influenced numerous top-tier leaders capable of steering companies to success. Bill Campbell's legacy was not a personal empire but an expanding network of talented minds he had shaped.

When you adopt the mindset of creating more leaders, you focus on empowerment. You share the skills, the insights, and the strategic perspectives that helped you rise. Rather than hoarding responsibility, you delegate meaningful tasks that stretch your people's abilities. You do not just assign routine duties; you assign real projects with consequences, allowing each person to experience the demands of decision-making. As they handle these challenges, they develop the confidence and competence to lead others in the future.

Moreover, you encourage initiative and critical thinking rather than blind obedience. Followers simply wait for orders. Emerging leaders, on the other hand, look for improvements, propose bold ideas, and take ownership of outcomes. That is precisely what you want in your team: individuals who are not content to wait for directions but actively seek better methods to achieve goals. If one of your team members eventually surpasses you in knowledge or skill, you have succeeded in creating a new leader who might carry the organisation or mission to heights you had not even imagined.

Investing in new leaders calls for a culture of trust. You cannot micromanage or guard your knowledge out of fear. Instead, you openly share techniques, experiences, both triumphs and failures, and give constructive feedback. Young leaders need both guidance and the room to stumble. Mistakes are part of the path to mastery. By patiently teaching them how to recover from errors, you develop resilience in the next generation of leaders. Over time, that resilience fortifies the entire organisation.

There is also an important psychological element at play. If people around you sense that you view them as mere followers, they might never aspire to step into leadership roles. Conversely, if they see you believe in their potential, treating them as future captains, they begin to adopt that mindset themselves. They rise to the occasion, often surprising even you with their capacity for responsibility. Leaders who stifle this growth stifle innovation, morale, and eventual succession plans.

Creating new leaders does not mean you relinquish your own authority. You remain a guiding presence, the central force that orchestrates efforts and upholds a clear direction. The difference is that you are not threatened by ambitious minds.

You welcome them, knowing that their success multiplies the overall impact you can have. By fostering an environment where emerging talent feels encouraged to assume greater control, you ensure that the organisation can thrive even if you step away. This is the essence of a lasting legacy.

Ultimately, you affirm your place in leadership history by how many individuals you have empowered to stand on their own. The leaders you develop will remember your influence, pass on your teachings, and build upon the structures you established. Your name might not appear in flashy headlines, but your influence will resonate in every decision they make, every team they shape, and every innovation they pioneer. If you want your leadership to endure, dedicate yourself to creating not just followers but a lineage of capable and ethical leaders. That is how you ensure your efforts outlive your tenure, leaving a footprint that cannot be erased by time.

2. The Power of Mentorship: Investing in the Next Generation

Mentorship is the bridge that carries your expertise and values to those who will steer the future. If you want your leadership legacy to be more than a fleeting chapter, you must commit to guiding the next generation. Mentorship is not merely about dispensing advice at random. It is a structured act of investing in emerging talent, forging a relationship that transforms raw potential into a focused force. When you mentor others, you are effectively ensuring that the knowledge, principles, and lessons you have gained over a lifetime do not vanish when you step aside.

One real-world figure who exemplifies the impact of mentorship is the late Wendy Kopp, founder of Teach For America. Although best known for mobilising graduates to teach in underprivileged communities, Kopp also focused on mentoring future leaders within her organisation. Instead of dictating all plans from above, she took emerging leaders under her wing, coaching them on how to run independent initiatives, refine their strategies, and tackle complex educational challenges. Over the years, many of her mentees went on to found their own educational ventures, extending Kopp's vision far beyond her direct reach.

In your role, mentorship must be intentional. Begin by identifying individuals who show promise, not only in skill but also in character. You look for those who display curiosity, diligence, and a genuine eagerness to learn. You do not limit yourself to those who are already top performers. Sometimes, the overlooked individual who works quietly behind the scenes might be the one who benefits most from your guidance. The key is spotting the spark that can ignite into a flame under the right mentorship.

Once you have identified potential mentees, arrange regular, structured sessions. These are not just for casual chats. A proper mentorship relationship involves goal-setting, accountability, and a willingness to address weaknesses. You might help your mentee map out career objectives, discuss specific challenges they are facing, and work together on skill-building. Make space for them to attempt new responsibilities. If they fall short, you debrief, discussing what went wrong and how to improve. This iterative process instils the grit and self-awareness needed for true leadership.

A mentor-mentee relationship also flourishes when you maintain transparency. Share your own lessons, including mistakes. It is tempting to show only your triumphant highlights, but that creates an unrealistic picture of leadership. By revealing instances where you erred, you teach your mentee how to handle adversity and recover. They realise that missteps do not define a leader's worth but can become stepping stones for stronger performance down the line.

Moreover, encourage your mentee to think critically rather than rely on your instructions. The goal is to shape an independent thinker who can operate effectively even without your guidance. Pose questions, offer multiple perspectives, and invite them to refine their own reasoning. Over time, you shift the dynamic so that they propose ideas, and you give your perspective on those proposals. This shift in the balance of conversation signals that they are growing into a leadership role themselves.

Another key facet is emotional support. Leadership can be isolating for new entrants. A mentee might wrestle with self-doubt, imposter syndrome, or anxiety about major responsibilities. A mentor who acknowledges these challenges, shares personal anecdotes of wrestling with similar feelings, and gives practical strategies for coping offers more than just professional advice. You become a stabilising presence who shows them that vulnerability does not negate strength.

Finally, a true mentor delights in seeing the mentee eventually surpass their own achievements. If you react with envy or fear when your protégé starts shining more brightly, you undermine the entire purpose of mentorship. Instead, celebrate it. That success demonstrates that the seeds you planted have grown into a thriving new branch of leadership. Through mentorship, you create an unbroken line of influence, passing down more than just business tactics. You hand over a moral compass and a sense of purposeful duty that your mentees will, in turn, pass on when they become mentors themselves.

3. Servant Leadership: Putting Others Before Yourself

In an era where everyone seems to clamber for the spotlight, choosing to serve first might appear counterintuitive. Yet servant leadership is rooted in a profound truth: the greatest power comes from uplifting others, not from hoarding status. When you adopt this style, you place the needs of your team, community, or cause at the forefront of your decisions. You uphold a higher principle than personal glory. Over time, you gain an authority that is far deeper than any official title. People give you their trust willingly because they see tangible evidence that your leadership is devoted to their welfare.

Robert K. Greenleaf, who popularised the term "servant leadership," often described it as the drive to ensure that other people's highest priorities are being served. That philosophy shaped Greenleaf's approach to corporate consulting and laid the foundation for numerous organisational development models. Servant leaders make it their task to expand autonomy, foster growth, and secure resources so that the entire group can flourish. This approach generates loyalty and propels consistent performance.

In your own leadership sphere, putting others first begins with understanding what they genuinely need. This demands that you listen more than you talk. Suppose you oversee a project team grappling with a tight deadline. Instead of dictating orders from above, ask each member where the biggest pain points are. Is it the software they are using. Is it conflicting priorities from another department. Is it a mismatch of skill sets for the tasks at hand. By taking their inputs seriously, you identify real obstacles and remove them rather than issuing general edicts that solve nothing.

A servant leader also commits to personal sacrifice for the collective good. This is not about playing the martyr. It is about being prepared to shoulder more risk or discomfort if it protects your team's morale or well-being. In practical terms, you might step in to handle a weekend emergency so that a stressed junior colleague can catch a break. Or you might decline a large personal bonus so the budget can fund training programmes for your entire division. These actions broadcast an unmistakable message: your priority is not personal gain but the welfare and development of those you lead.

This mindset carries over into decision-making. When faced with a trade-off between efficiency and employee support, you strike a balance that does not sacrifice the human element on the altar of short-term profit. For instance, if budget cuts are inevitable, you look for creative alternatives before resorting to layoffs. Or, if you must lay people off, you offer fair severance and help them transition to new opportunities. A leader who acts with compassion, even in harsh times, gains a reputation for loyalty that can strengthen an organisation's culture.

Servant leadership extends beyond your immediate team. It involves community impact. You might volunteer time, resources, or expertise to uplift local charities or educational programmes. When your team sees you act selflessly in that wider context, it reminds them that leadership is about service at every level. Instead of fixating on personal ambition, you sow the seeds of generosity. The culture that results tends to spur higher engagement because people take pride in working under a leader who cares about the bigger picture.

At times, you will face sceptics who see selflessness as weakness. However, consistent servant leadership disproves that assumption. By empowering people rather than subjugating them, you create a united force that hits targets more reliably. By minimising ego, you encourage straightforward communication and reduce political friction. This synergy often leads to a performance boost that purely self-centred leaders cannot match. The irony is that, by prioritising others, you often achieve better results than those fixated on personal success.

Ultimately, servant leadership is not about casting yourself as a doormat. You remain decisive and strong-willed. But every choice aligns with the question: "Will this strengthen my team and those we serve, or is it simply feeding my own desires." When you live by that question, you transform leadership into something more than a pursuit of authority. You create a ripple effect of service-mindedness, turning ordinary groups into resilient communities driven by shared purpose. In doing so, you solidify a legacy that echoes well beyond your direct realm of influence.

4. How to Leave a Legacy That Outlives You

Real leadership transcends personal ambition. If you want to forge a legacy that stands solid long after you have left, you must design your efforts to continue bearing fruit without your constant hand on the helm. This demands more than short-term achievements or flashy accolades. It requires stable structures, embedded values, and a culture that encourages perpetual growth.

A classic illustration of a long-lasting legacy is found in the story of Lee Kuan Yew, Singapore's first Prime Minister. Under his guidance, Singapore transformed from a struggling trading port into a prosperous economic powerhouse. Lee Kuan Yew did not simply rule. He invested heavily in education, infrastructure, and a robust governance framework designed to function well beyond his own tenure. Although his leadership style generated debate, the infrastructural, social, and economic pillars he set in motion have endured for decades, shaping Singapore into one of the world's most advanced nations. That outcome did not rest on his personality, but on the institutional bedrock, he established.

To build something that lasts, you should start by articulating a clear vision that is not purely about you. Others must see themselves in that vision. If your plan is overly personal, centred on your image or dependent on your unique talents, its impact may wane once you step aside. Instead, shape a mission that appeals to universal aspirations. Whether you want to revolutionise healthcare, modernise education, or create a forward-thinking tech environment, frame it so future stakeholders can adopt and adapt it.

Next, establish systems that do not rely on your daily input. Document processes, create guidelines for decision-making, and decentralise authority where suitable. If you run a non-profit, ensure that its funding mechanisms, governance structures, and volunteer management protocols can function smoothly, even if you are no longer involved. If you manage a business, foster a leadership pipeline that consistently trains new managers and invests in their development. This pipeline approach means the culture you have built does not evaporate once the main figurehead is absent.

Culture is crucial. A high-performing environment is one thing, but a principled and high-performing environment is the gold standard. Engage your team in defining the shared values that guide how they treat customers, collaborate with each other, and handle conflicts. Embed those values into hiring, performance reviews, and everyday recognition. If you leave behind a culture that people cherish and protect, they will keep living it out, ensuring continuity of your influence. This culture becomes your signature, even if your name is no longer on the office door.

Part of leaving a lasting legacy also involves ensuring financial and structural stability. Flamboyant expansions or big-ticket items might bring you praise initially, but they can burden successors if the finances are shaky. Instead, aim for prudent growth and sustainable strategies. If you are funding a scholarship programme or a new departmental branch, plan how it will sustain itself through future economic cycles. That might include endowments, partnerships, or diversified revenue streams. A fortress built on a fragile foundation will crumble once the environment shifts.

Do not underestimate the role of storytelling. Document the organisation's journey, the hurdles you overcame, and the rationale behind your major decisions. Write down both successes and missteps in a transparent fashion. This narrative can act as a guiding text for those who come after you. When new leaders understand the original spirit behind a strategy or policy, they can refine it for new challenges without losing the principles you championed.

Finally, ensure that the people around you are ready to step into larger shoes. Invest personally in their growth. Push them to enhance their public speaking, financial acumen, or negotiation abilities. Involve them in key discussions rather than locking them out. You might even consider forming a formal leadership council that gradually learns to run entire segments of the operation without your oversight. By the time you are ready to step back, they can carry on seamlessly, and your legacy will unfold through their actions, not just your memory.

A legacy that outlives you is not an accident. It is built on deliberate structure, inclusive vision, and a culture that resonates with core values you have championed all along. By setting up these pillars carefully, you give your mission a life independent of your own presence. Your name might one day fade from the headlines, but the practices, institutions, and leaders you leave behind will keep driving progress. That is the mark of a leader who truly thought ahead and built a future that can stand on its own feet.

5. The Final Test of Leadership: Stepping Away with Honour

Every leader faces a moment when it is time to step aside. The reason may vary: retirement, a new pursuit, or ensuring that fresh energy takes the reins. This transition can be more daunting than any earlier challenge. Your influence, identity, and day-to-day purpose might feel intertwined with your leadership role. Yet, leaving the stage gracefully and ensuring continuity for those who follow can be the ultimate test of your maturity and integrity.

A standout example comes from Ratan Tata, who chaired the Tata Group, one of India's largest conglomerates. During his tenure, he oversaw expansions into global markets, launched innovative products like the Tata Nano, and fostered a strong culture of ethics and philanthropy. At the time of his retirement, he did not cling to power or attempt to micromanage from behind the scenes. Instead, he chose a successor, Cyrus Mistry, and stepped away to allow new leadership to flourish. Although corporate drama later unfolded, Ratan Tata's initial decision to relinquish control showcased his willingness to pass on responsibility. His exit was a demonstration that he understood the group's strength lay in a structured transition, not his permanent presence.

When your turn arrives, plan your departure carefully. Begin by grooming your replacement, ideally someone who has been tested by challenging roles and mentored under your wing. If your organisation has a formal succession framework, follow it closely. If not, create one well in advance. Give your successor genuine authority to shape decisions before you leave. That real-life practice under your watchful but not overbearing eye will refine their readiness. Your departure does not become a shock but a natural handover.

Transparency is critical. Announce your plans to step down with enough lead time for everyone to adapt. Keep the lines of communication open. This helps prevent anxiety or speculation about the organisation's future. If you vanish without warning, people can feel rudderless. By giving them clarity, you preserve stability and maintain confidence in the institution's resilience.

You will also need to address your own emotional journey. Leadership can be addictive, especially if you have identified strongly with your role. Letting go might stir anxiety or a sense of loss. Prepare mentally by revisiting the broader purpose of your life. You are more than the position you hold. Reflect on the other contributions you can make, whether through mentorship, philanthropy, or personal endeavours. By mapping out your post-leadership life, you ease the transition

The Legacy Of A Leader: Mentorship And Impact

and reduce the urge to meddle in the affairs of your former domain.

Moreover, resist the temptation to meddle once your successor is in place. If they consult you, offer your perspective, but do not impose. Publicly support them, even if they make decisions you would not have chosen. Stepping away honourably means giving them room to lead, to make errors, and to grow. If you hover like a shadow, you undermine their authority. A strong organisation must learn to function without you. That is how your legacy becomes self-sustaining rather than dependent on your ongoing presence.

Thank those who have walked alongside you, your team, your partners, even your critics who sharpened your thinking. Recognition builds goodwill and encourages others to uphold the values you instilled. When people see you parting on good terms, they feel a sense of closure and readiness for the new leadership chapter. They also remember your final act as one of generosity and respect, reinforcing the positive impression you leave behind.

Finally, reflect on the journey. A graceful exit is not about retreating in defeat. It is about concluding a chapter with heads held high. You have contributed ideas, shaped policies, and raised capable individuals who can keep advancing the mission. This is not the end of your leadership but the beginning of a new role, one where your influence might be more indirect but still vital. You shift from centre stage to a supportive vantage point, ready to offer wisdom when asked while trusting that the seeds you planted will flourish in your absence.

Leaving with honour shows that your leadership was never about feeding your own ego or clinging to power. It was about serving a cause greater than yourself. If you can step away with dignity, setting up the next wave of leaders for success, you confirm that your legacy stands on a firm foundation. You prove that real leaders know when to bow out and let the future unfold under fresh guidance. That, in itself, cements your place as a legend in the eyes of those you once led.

Conclusion

Your legacy is the invisible thread that binds your leadership to the future. In these pages, you have seen that great leaders do not aspire to gather crowds of obedient followers but to build a cadre of confident decision-makers who can continue the mission. You have uncovered the essence of mentorship, which is not sporadic or superficial but an investment in shaping capable minds and strong characters. You have examined the selfless nature of true leadership, placing others first, ensuring their growth, and creating conditions for them to surpass your achievements. You have explored how to anchor a lasting impact through robust systems and a culture that thrives independently. And you have faced the final test: stepping away when your chapter is complete, entrusting the legacy to the stewards you have prepared.

Every move you make in leadership, whether large or small, contributes a piece to that legacy. By striving to create new leaders, you extend your influence across generations. By mentoring with sincerity and depth, you multiply your effect through the people you guide. By serving before seeking your own interests, you install a moral framework that compels loyalty and respect. By constructing sustainable structures and an inspiring culture, you give your mission the stamina to flourish when you are gone. And by departing with honour, you show that your dedication was never about clinging to power but about real, transformative progress.

Embrace this vision of leadership. Use your position not just to command but to elevate those in your orbit. If you nurture emerging talents, serve them rather than exploit them, and carefully set the stage for an enduring positive impact, you have uncovered the essence of real leadership. The baton you pass to the next generation carries your ideals, your wisdom, and your accomplishments. In that handover, you expand your legacy from a single lifetime to a legacy that echoes long after your physical presence fades. That is how leaders who understand the meaning of honour truly endure.

CHAPTER 9

The Leadership Paradoxes: The Hidden Secrets Of Great Leaders

You might think leadership is all about standing at the front, commanding respect, and wielding undeniable power. Yet, if you strip away the glamour, you find that true leadership is full of surprising contradictions. You see individuals who guide entire movements by humbling themselves or those who gain power by stepping back. You watch disciplined leaders who appear rigid yet unlock a sense of freedom others never achieve. You come across people with no formal rank who still direct opinions, choices, and even policy. These are the paradoxes that define exceptional leadership.

In this chapter, you will discover five core paradoxes that define the hidden truths of great leaders. You will see why the willingness to follow gives you the insight needed to lead with authenticity. You will learn how showing your weak points can actually strengthen the bonds of trust. You will understand the connection between discipline and freedom and why letting go of certain controls can ignite deeper commitment in your team.

Finally, you will see how the absence of an official title does not diminish genuine influence. Each paradox forces you to question standard assumptions about leadership and might push you to adopt fresh perspectives in your own journey.

1. Lead by Following: The Wisdom of Lifelong Learning

You may think that being a leader means always taking the initiative, always having the final say, and always directing others. Yet one of the most powerful secrets of sustained leadership is the ability to follow first. This paradox says that if you are truly wise, you never graduate from learning. Instead, you keep seeking perspectives beyond your own, approaching mentors with curiosity, and remaining open to ideas that challenge your assumptions. By doing so, you gain the understanding that fuels genuine authority.

A stark illustration comes from Robert Baden-Powell, the British Army officer who founded the Scouting movement. Before establishing a global organisation that shaped young lives, he spent years observing the daily habits of front-line soldiers and local guides during military campaigns. He did not rush in as an aloof commander. He spent time following practical advice from those on the ground. He learned survival tricks, pathfinding, and relationship-building from individuals who were not high-ranking but had direct, tangible knowledge. By adopting a follower's mindset, he gathered insights that later formed the basis of Scouting's outdoor education ethos. The success of that movement rested on Baden-Powell's readiness to learn before he led.

In your life, you can unlock this paradox by deliberately choosing moments to yield the spotlight and listen. Whether you are in a meeting or running a project, identify someone with expertise or a viewpoint you lack. Hand them the platform. Ask them probing questions. Let them shape your thinking. This does not mean you downplay your own knowledge. It means you recognise that your own perspective, no matter how informed, is never the full picture. When you step into a follower's shoes, you gather a more accurate map of the terrain. Your final decisions carry more weight because they account for factors you might have missed in isolation.

Another dimension of leading by following is humility in mentorship relationships. Select someone you respect, perhaps a seasoned colleague, a retired executive in your field, or even a rising star who brings an entirely new perspective, and request their guidance. Share your challenges openly. Resist the temptation to show off your successes. Focus on the gaps you want to fill. This approach boosts your growth in two ways: first, you harvest real expertise; second, you demonstrate that you value knowledge more than pride. People who see that you are willing to learn often trust you more because they sense your commitment to accuracy and depth, not just self-image.

Adopting a follower's mindset can also break echo chambers. If you only lead, you might filter out dissenting voices, whether consciously or not. If you make it a habit to follow in certain contexts by reading broadly, attending workshops beyond your usual domain, or seeking peer review of your ideas, you expose yourself to critiques and alternatives. This keeps your leadership fresh. You avoid becoming outdated or trapped in past successes that no longer apply to present challenges.

Some worry that showing a follower's posture dilutes their authority. In reality, the opposite is often true. When your team witnesses you listening and learning, they see a leader who is not driven by ego. This encourages them to share insights more freely, confident that you will not dismiss or belittle them. Over time, your credibility grows because your decisions are informed and your approach is inclusive. You become the leader people consult voluntarily, not the one they merely obey.

This paradox, leading by following, boils down to lifelong learning. You never announce that you have learned enough, nor do you fear seeking help when you face novel problems. Such a stance keeps you agile in a fast-changing world. It also nurtures the humility that staves off arrogance. By preserving that beginner's mind, you stay open to the spark of innovation that might come from the most unexpected sources. In the end, those who can follow with grace find their leadership roots grow deeper and more resilient. They stand firm in a world of shifting sands because they have anchored themselves in wisdom gathered from every corner.

2. Strength Through Vulnerability: Why Admitting Mistakes Builds Trust

You have been taught to keep a stiff upper lip, appear unshakeable, and project flawless confidence. Yet, one of the most effective ways to strengthen your position as a leader is to show vulnerability. This does not mean complaining without end or wallowing in self-doubt. Instead, it involves admitting that you are human, acknowledging your errors, and granting your team permission to do the same. Though it might look like a crack in your armour, vulnerability can forge a stronger bond than an unblemished facade ever could.

A well-documented case involves Indra Nooyi's handling of a product-launch mishap during her time at PepsiCo. Faced with disappointing sales figures, Nooyi did not pretend the data was rosy. She openly shared the missteps made in market research and admitted that the leadership team, herself included, had overlooked signals from consumers. That honesty prompted a shift in strategy that welcomed fresh input from junior staff and external focus groups. The renewed approach eventually led to a revamped product line that performed well. Nooyi's vulnerability did not erode her credibility. It enhanced it, as employees felt comfortable raising concerns, and managers re-evaluated decisions with fewer blind spots.

When you show vulnerability, you send a powerful message: "I trust you enough to reveal my imperfections." In a world where leaders often hide behind polished veneers, genuine openness stands out. It invites your team to respond in kind. They become more inclined to admit their own shortcomings rather than hide them. This transparency accelerates problem-solving. Rather than scrambling to cover up an error, people promptly voice the issue and look for ways to fix it. The entire group moves faster because it is not weighed down by fear of exposure.

Vulnerability can also strengthen loyalty. If you consistently present yourself as untouchable and unflawed, you risk creating distance. Your team might respect your skill but never feel personally connected to you. On the other hand, when you reveal that you, too, can slip up, you become more relatable. People root for someone who shows human qualities rather than an ivory-tower figure who seems beyond their realm of experience. This bond can mean the difference between a staff member working for a pay cheque and one who goes the extra mile out of genuine devotion.

Of course, vulnerability must be balanced. You do not want to spill every worry or fear across your organisation, creating chaos or undermining confidence. Targeted vulnerability is key. Share enough detail so your people see your humanity, but maintain composure in how you address solutions. For instance, if you have miscalculated a timeline, admit it calmly, outline the lessons learned, and lay out a new schedule. This way, you transform an error into a stepping stone for collective progress rather than a meltdown that leaves everyone on edge.

Research from the London-based Corporate Leadership Council notes that teams guided by leaders who own their mistakes tend to have higher trust levels and improved job satisfaction. Mistakes, when addressed openly, become teaching moments rather than career-ending catastrophes. This fosters an environment where innovation can flourish because staff are not paralysed by the dread of slip-ups. They understand that a misstep, if acknowledged and corrected, becomes a valuable piece of the learning curve.

Your willingness to show vulnerability also sets a moral example. It conveys that integrity matters more than image. Those under your guidance see that you prioritise truth over appearances. As a result, they mirror that honesty in their dealings, which can improve customer relations, product quality, and overall workplace culture.

In a paradoxical way, vulnerability is a form of power. By casting aside the illusion of perfection, you create a space where genuine dialogue emerges. You become someone people can confide in, collaborate with, and rally around. Instead of chipping away at your authority, the admission of your human side cements your role as a leader who values growth over ego. It is not a sign of weakness. It is a testament to the inner strength that can withstand scrutiny without resorting to concealment.

3. More Discipline, More Freedom: How Structure Creates Success

It sounds contradictory at first: how can imposing discipline result in greater freedom. Yet, top-performing leaders know that when you establish clear standards and routines, you remove guesswork and confusion. This creates space for creativity, agility, and personal growth. You might expect discipline to stifle spontaneity, but the opposite usually unfolds. Structured environments give you the focus to excel without constant chaos.

You see an excellent example in the life of Admiral Grace Hopper, a pioneer in computer programming for the US Navy. Hopper was known for her unwavering discipline, waking up early to tackle the day's objectives, insisting on organised data protocols, and enforcing precise coding standards among her teams. Critics might have deemed it rigid, but the outcome was groundbreaking innovation. By adhering to strict guidelines, her developers avoided sloppy mistakes and wasted time. They had more space for big leaps in logic, eventually leading to programming advances that shaped modern computing. Her style epitomised the idea that disciplined execution frees the mind to explore deeper creativity.

In your own setting, discipline can take many forms. You might run daily stand-up meetings at a set time, ensuring that the team synchronises goals and addresses obstacles right away. These short, consistent gatherings minimise fragmentation later. You might institute a robust project management system that tracks tasks and deadlines meticulously. Far from strangling spontaneity, this structure prevents the random drifts that drain time and energy. Because tasks are tracked, you avoid spending valuable hours chasing status updates or deciphering unclear targets. That saved energy can then fuel imaginative strategies and thoughtful problem-solving.

Discipline also means setting personal boundaries. You create blocks of deep work time, during which distractions and idle chatter are off-limits. You commit to finishing tasks on schedule, not dragging them out across indefinite stretches. This approach does not transform you into a dull automaton. Rather, it grants you the satisfaction of moving from one achievement to the next without the stress of half-done projects nagging at your mind. Once the vital work is done, you can afford real downtime where you unwind fully, free from the guilt that you are neglecting essential duties.

Teams respond well to disciplined leadership because it provides clarity. Everyone understands the rules of engagement, the standards of performance, and the penalties for shirking responsibilities. There is less finger-pointing and more unity because the expectations are transparent and fair. When conflicts arise, you can resolve them by referencing the agreed-upon framework rather than resorting to subjective opinions. This reduces tension and promotes a sense of justice within the group.

Another outcome is that discipline supports consistent improvement. You track performance metrics, hold regular reviews, and address shortfalls immediately. This feedback loop creates a culture of continuous growth. People know they cannot rest on past achievements. Instead, they refine skills, adapt to new tools, or learn emerging best practices. Over time, the team evolves into a highly capable unit that handles challenges with confident efficiency. This efficiency, ironically, affords you greater leeway to experiment with fresh ideas because you trust the foundational routines to keep the train on track.

Some fear discipline will strip away all joy, but the reality is far more positive. Strict guidelines can free you from decision fatigue. If you wake up daily and follow a proven routine, you remove the burden of making trivial choices. Your mental bandwidth remains available for the tougher strategic calls. It is the same reason many successful leaders adopt consistent morning habits, structured work calendars, or standardised protocols for repeated tasks. By automating the mundane, they leave room for purposeful thinking.

You might worry about pushing discipline too far, and that risk exists. Excessive micromanagement can demoralise a team. The key is balance. You establish routines that address recurring needs but grant individuals enough autonomy to inject creativity where it matters. The best approach is to articulate core expectations, like deadlines, reporting structures, quality benchmarks, and then allow people the freedom to choose how they meet those standards. This fusion of structure and independence fosters a resilient, empowered workforce.

In the end, discipline leads to freedom by giving you a stable platform on which you can innovate and explore. You do not get bogged down in crisis management or half-finished tasks. Instead, you run a well-oiled operation that liberates you to pursue bigger ideas and bolder initiatives. By embracing consistent rules, you ironically discover the headroom needed to break boundaries. This paradox underscores why real leaders place as much emphasis on consistent execution as they do on visionary thinking.

4. Control vs. Trust: Knowing When to Let Go

If you are in a leadership role, the impulse to keep your hands on every lever can be overwhelming. After all, you carry the ultimate responsibility for outcomes. Yet, great leaders know that an iron grip on every detail can suffocate talent and stifle growth. The paradox here is that by relinquishing a measure of control, you often gain deeper commitment, initiative, and ownership from your team. This does not mean you let chaos reign. It means you carefully calibrate when to step back and when to stay involved.

A revealing example is Bill Walsh's approach during his time as head coach of the San Francisco 49ers. Walsh introduced a strategic framework known as the "Standard of Performance," which laid out clear expectations for every role on the team. He drilled the fundamentals relentlessly but then trusted his players to interpret the playbook on the field. Quarterbacks had leeway to adjust tactics based on real-time conditions rather than waiting for instructions from the sidelines. That freedom nurtured leadership qualities in the players themselves. Under Walsh's blend of structure and trust, the 49ers claimed multiple Super Bowl titles. His reputation remains legendary in the NFL, showing how strategic delegation can spark extraordinary results.

In your context, you balance control and trust by first setting clear objectives and boundaries. Make sure your team understands the end goal, the available resources, and any non-negotiable constraints. Then, give them room to operate. Resist the urge to hover and micromanage. Check in periodically, not obsessively. Clarify that they can approach you if they need guidance, but you will not watch their every move. This arrangement feels strange if you are used to pulling every string, yet it allows team members to develop problem-solving skills and to feel genuine pride in their contributions.

Trust can also prompt creative solutions that never surface under close supervision. If employees worry you will override their suggestions anyway, they are unlikely to propose novel approaches. By giving them autonomy, you invite their innovative spark. They might redesign a process, discover a fresh angle in marketing, or spot a hidden efficiency. You position yourself not just as a boss but as a facilitator who orchestrates a wide range of talents. Over time, your collective capacity grows exponentially as each member leans into their strengths.

Another benefit of trusting your people is that you create a deeper sense of loyalty. Autonomy is a psychological driver. Most professionals crave the chance to exercise their judgment. When you demonstrate that you trust their capabilities, they repay you by striving to exceed expectations. It becomes a cycle: more trust yields higher motivation, which fosters better performance, which justifies continued trust. If you hold on too tight, you disrupt that positive cycle, leaving you with a team of order-takers rather than self-driven contributors.

That said, letting go does not mean ignoring warning signs. You remain vigilant, especially for mission-critical assignments. Have checkpoints and progress markers so you can confirm that work stays on track. If problems emerge, do not swoop in with condescension. Offer guidance, help identify the root cause, and adjust course collaboratively. This approach retains accountability but avoids heavy-handed control that strangles the team's initiative.

There is a psychological hurdle, too. It can feel risky to entrust others with what you normally do yourself. You may worry about your authority or fear that errors will reflect poorly on you. Yet the long-term harm of hoarding control is far greater. You drain your own capacity by micromanaging, and you deny your team the chance to evolve. If you do not nurture their abilities, you ultimately create a single point of failure: yourself.

Trust is not blind faith. It is earned and maintained through consistent performance and open communication. You start small, assigning manageable tasks and observing how people handle them. As their competence grows, you grant wider latitude. You also cultivate a culture that praises initiative and punishes dishonesty, not honest mistakes. Over time, trust becomes woven into every relationship, elevating your collective resilience.

In the end, the paradox of control versus trust demands self-discipline. Your authority is undeniable, but that does not mean you should use it at full force every second. The more effectively you distribute responsibility, the more everyone invests in the shared mission. That dynamic synergy can catapult your team to achievements you could not single-handedly deliver. By stepping back and trusting others, you empower them to step up, and that is where extraordinary leadership emerges.

5. Leading Without a Title: Influence Beyond Position

Many assume you can only lead if you carry a lofty title: Director, CEO, or Manager. Yet, true leadership extends far beyond formal rank. People who hold no grand role often wield significant influence in shaping opinions, fuelling morale, or driving change. This paradox reveals that genuine authority springs not just from position but from the respect and trust earned by who you are and what you do.

You see this principle at work in the career of Mo Salah, the professional footballer from Egypt. Although not always wearing the captain's armband at Liverpool or on the Egyptian national team, his leadership emerges on and off the pitch through his consistent performance, humility, and charitable actions. He encourages younger players, sets a high standard in training, and shows composure under immense scrutiny.

While the official title might rest with someone else, many look to Salah for guidance, inspiration, and an example of how to handle pressure with grace. His case shows that your influence need not hinge on an official badge of authority.

If you want to lead without a title, you start by mastering your role. Whatever your assignment, carry it out with excellence. Show reliability by meeting deadlines, solving problems, and supporting others who need a hand. Your quiet competence will not go unnoticed. Colleagues begin to consult you, not because you have a managerial label, but because they trust your capability and consistency.

Another element is fostering relationships across departments or social circles. Leaders who rely on position alone might command compliance but fail to spark genuine collaboration. By building rapport informally, sharing insights, providing helpful introductions, or even giving morale-boosting comments, you establish yourself as someone who unifies. As your network expands, so does your capacity to influence. People from varied areas begin to see you as a linchpin, someone who can connect the dots and guide them to better outcomes.

Effective communication also propels you. You do not need an executive suite to speak up in meetings or to propose bold new ideas. If your points are well-researched and delivered with clarity, they hold weight. Over time, colleagues and even superiors learn to value your input. You become a thought leader within the organisation, shaping strategies even if your name does not appear at the top of the org chart.

Integrity remains essential. When you lack a formal title, trust is your currency. If you promise something, follow through. If you see unethical behaviour, address it promptly, even if you must do so discreetly. Uphold transparency and fairness when you collaborate. People gravitate towards those who show moral reliability. They back your ideas because they believe in your character, not because they fear your rank.

You also demonstrate emotional intelligence. Leading informally often involves guiding individuals who owe you no direct obligation. If you push too hard or attempt to bully them, they can easily walk away. This means you must tune in to their motivations, fears, and personal ambitions. By aligning your requests or proposals with their goals, you encourage them to join your cause voluntarily. This skilful persuasion fosters unity and a sense of shared ownership, both hallmarks of real leadership.

When obstacles arise, an untitled leader can still respond decisively. Maybe the team hits a technical snag. If you know a possible solution or a relevant expert to consult, you make it happen. You do not hide behind the excuse of lacking authority. You step forward, share your plan, and rally others to get it done. This can transform you into a go-to figure whenever crises emerge, effectively increasing your influence in subsequent issues.

At some point, you may gain an official title. But by then, your leadership will not rely on it. You will already be the person people trust due to your proven track record, empathy, and collaborative spirit. That is the best scenario because you step into formal authority with a strong foundation of goodwill. Conversely, if you never receive a fancy title, your impact remains intact. A quiet influencer can shape hearts and minds in remarkable ways, forging breakthroughs that official hierarchies often struggle to deliver.

In the end, leadership without a title rests on example, service, and genuine connection. You become the individual who lights the path, not by commanding from on high, but by stepping alongside your peers and guiding them through action. This paradox underscores the highest truth: real leadership is not bestowed; it is earned through the everyday decisions you make. If you learn to lead from where you stand, you might accomplish more than any formal position could promise.

Conclusion

Paradoxes can feel puzzling at first glance, but each hidden truth illuminates a path to higher effectiveness and authenticity. You have seen why you become a stronger leader by following first, why vulnerability cements trust rather than undermining it, how more discipline can produce true freedom, and why loosening your grip can yield greater initiative from your team. Finally, you discovered that real influence does not require a title; it emerges from your example, your relationships, and the reputation you build through consistent actions.

These paradoxes challenge standard assumptions about leadership. They remind you that power and humility can walk side by side and that boundaries can create more, not less, creativity. They teach you to see beyond formal structures, realising that authority anchored in respect often surpasses any badge of office. If you embrace these insights, you unlock a dimension of leadership that is both surprising and transformative. Rather than battling these contradictions, incorporate them into your style, and you will find your influence growing deeper and more enduring.

CHAPTER 10

The Leadership Code: Your Personal Blueprint For Success

You have ascended the mountain of leadership principles, from self-mastery and mindset to the art of influence and the crucible of crisis. You have uncovered the hidden paradoxes that define the greatest leaders in history. And now you stand on the pinnacle, poised to write your own chapter in the grand story of leadership. This final stage is not about gathering more theories. It is about integrating all you have learned into a personal blueprint that will guide your decisions, shape your conduct, and ignite your potential to inspire others.

In this last chapter, you will construct your leadership philosophy and forge a personal code of honour. You will explore how to safeguard your values in the heat of conflict and stress, ensuring that no external force can shatter your moral bearings. You will discover the daily rituals that keep legendary leaders focused, energised, and ready for challenges.

You will then take the final step, embedding these lessons into your life so that your pursuit of leadership greatness becomes a daily walk, not a one-time event. This is your moment to gather every insight, every lesson and transform them into a living, breathing code that will elevate you and those you serve for years to come.

1. Creating Your Own Leadership Philosophy

A leadership philosophy is your guiding framework, the mental architecture that shapes how you interact with people, make decisions, and measure success. It is not a list of slogans scribbled on a notepad. It is a belief system that weaves all your experiences, lessons, and convictions into a cohesive approach to leading others. When you have a well-defined philosophy, you no longer react to events chaotically. You respond from a centre of clarity that directs every choice you make.

Before you can craft this philosophy, take stock of the insights you have gathered on your journey so far. You have learned the power of self-leadership: how discipline, emotional control, and consistent habits build the foundation for guiding others. You have delved into the mindset of humility, resilience, and vision. You have understood the nature of influence, why it rests on trust, integrity, and a willingness to serve. You have grappled with decision-making under pressure, tested yourself in times of crisis, and come to see that real leadership is about forging more leaders, not mere followers. Each of these lessons can form a strand in the overarching system you will call your leadership philosophy.

To begin, isolate your core beliefs about people and the nature of teamwork. Do you hold that individuals perform best when given autonomy and high standards, or do you believe they need close guidance until they mature. Are you convinced that honesty should be absolute, or do you allow for strategic omissions. There is no universal template here, but clarity is key. Write these beliefs in plain language. If you catch yourself using lofty buzzwords, translate them into terms that resonate with real-life situations. When you

The Leadership Code: Your Personal Blueprint For Success

articulate them simply, you can apply them under pressure without confusion.

Next, decide how you define success in leadership. Is it about boosting profits, expanding reach, or shaping a positive culture. Perhaps you aim to unite people in a shared cause that outlasts any single project. Be precise. Success metrics guide your actions. If you measure triumph by how well you elevate your team's morale, you will prioritise mentoring and transparent communication. If you measure it by community impact, you will invest in service initiatives and alliances outside your immediate circle. Your definition of success colours every goal you set.

Reflect also on your stance regarding risks and failures. Do you believe in a bold approach that embraces experimentation, or do you lean towards careful analysis. A solid leadership philosophy includes a position on how to handle setbacks. If you see failure as a crucial teacher, you will build a culture where mistakes spark innovation rather than fear. If you treat failure as something to hide at all costs, you risk creating an environment of anxiety and underachievement. The more candid you are about your attitude to risk, the more consistent your team will find you in tough times.

Another element is how you view power and hierarchy. Are you convinced that strict structures are vital for clarity, or do you prefer flattened hierarchies where everyone's voice matters equally. Perhaps you favour a hybrid model with clear leadership but active encouragement of input from all levels. Spell out your reasoning. Your stand on power distribution shapes the daily dynamics of your group. If you are consistent, people know what to expect, and you avoid abrupt shifts that derail trust.

Finally, remember to keep your philosophy flexible. As you gain fresh experiences or face new environments, you may refine certain views. However, the fundamentals, your moral code, and your sense of purpose should remain unshaken. This balance of firm ideals and adaptable methods is what keeps a leadership philosophy relevant in changing times. If you hold on too rigidly to details, you become blind to evolving circumstances. If you drift without a core, you surrender your identity. Finding that equilibrium is what transforms abstract ideas into an operational creed.

When you have outlined these aspects, your beliefs about people, your measures of success, your stance on risk, your understanding of power, and your readiness to adapt, you have the bones of a personal leadership philosophy. Put it all into writing. Read it aloud to yourself. Test it against imaginary scenarios. The goal is not to craft a perfect document but to forge a statement of intent that you can live by. Once you have this blueprint, leading becomes more than a set of ad-hoc decisions. It becomes a deliberate act of living in alignment with your deepest convictions.

2. Developing a Personal Code of Honour

A personal code of honour is more than an abstract desire to be "good." It is a deliberate set of ethical commitments that you pledge to uphold, regardless of the cost. This code is the shield that protects your integrity when shortcuts beckon. It is the lodestar you consult when external voices push you to compromise. And it is the standard by which you judge your own conduct when no one else is watching. In a world where moral lines are frequently blurred, having a code of honour is what keeps you steady through the storms.

First, examine the values that resonate most with your deeper self. Some leaders hold unwavering honesty at the core.

Others centre on fairness, loyalty, courage, or compassion. You may identify a handful of guiding principles that encompass who you want to be in both public and private spheres. Avoid copying someone else's code. If it does not reflect your genuine beliefs, it will collapse under stress. Instead, let your real convictions emerge. Maybe you decide that transparency, kindness, and perseverance form your triad of priorities. Or perhaps duty, discipline, and respect define your moral axis. Tailor it to what truly matters to you.

Once you have these key values, translate them into behaviours. It is not enough to say, "I value loyalty." You need to define what that means in practice. For instance, you might state, "I will never undermine my colleagues behind their backs" or "I will defend someone who is unfairly attacked, even if it is risky." By anchoring values in concrete actions, you remove ambiguity. Your code of honour becomes a roadmap, guiding you toward specific ethical decisions when uncertainties arise. If your code says, "I uphold honesty in all dealings," that means you do not fudge numbers, hide mistakes, or withhold critical information. It might feel more challenging to keep such promises, but the clarity they provide is priceless.

Consider potential dilemmas you might face. A bribe from a contractor. Pressure from superiors to cover up subpar results. An enticing partnership that conflicts with your civic or family responsibilities. Spell out your stance on these scenarios now, in the calm before the storm. When crisis strikes, you can consult your code rather than flounder in confusion. This preparation arms you with moral readiness. You have already rehearsed your response in your mind, and you know what your standards demand. You will not be paralysed by indecision when time is scarce.

Of course, no code of honour is effective if you treat it like a dusty relic once written. Revisit it regularly. Reflect on recent challenges and ask if you upheld or drifted from your code. If you faltered, analyse why. Was the pressure too sudden. Were you unsure of the correct action. Adjust your code if you find overlooked areas, but do not discard it at the first sign of tension. The code only becomes genuine when you fight to uphold it in real conflicts.

It also helps to share your code with a trusted friend, mentor, or confidant. Let them know the ideals you strive to embody. Encourage them to call you out if they see you straying. This level of accountability can be humbling, but it cements your resolve. You essentially declare that your honour is not negotiable and that you welcome reminders if your actions slip below your proclaimed standard.

Living by a personal code of honour demands sacrifice. At times you might forfeit a lucrative deal, lose fleeting popularity, or even face hostility for refusing to compromise. But that cost is a small price for preserving your self-respect and maintaining the trust of those who look up to you. In fact, the more you stand by your principles under duress, the more your reputation as a leader of integrity grows. People sense that you are not swayed by convenience or immediate gains, and this reliability forms the bedrock of long-term loyalty.

Ultimately, your personal code of honour is the anchor of your leadership identity. It ensures your external achievements do not come at the expense of your inner moral compass. By committing to it daily, you transform lofty ideals into lived reality. The result is a leadership style infused with sincerity, courage, and the consistent respect of peers and followers alike.

3. How to Stay True to Your Values Under Pressure

Holding to your beliefs is straightforward in theory. It is when everything is on the line, your livelihood, your reputation, or your team's morale, that your resolve is truly tested. Pressurised environments can tempt even the most upright individual to bend ethical lines or abandon their convictions for quick gains. To remain steady under such strain, you must be prepared both mentally and practically. You cannot expect your values to defend themselves. You have to stand guard.

The first step is acknowledging that adversity will come. This mindset removes the element of surprise. If you believe you will never be challenged, you might cave when trouble arrives unexpectedly. By anticipating the storms, you train yourself to see difficulties as tests rather than random misfortunes. This shift in perspective makes you more alert and ready to respond with clarity. When an associate pressures you to fudge a report or sign off on a questionable deal, you are not caught off-guard. You already know such scenarios can happen, and you approach them with the armour of foresight.

Next, practise scenario planning. Visualise situations where your values might conflict with external demands. Imagine you run a consultancy and a prospective client offers you a huge contract but insists you downplay certain facts in your analysis. Or suppose you manage a healthcare facility, and budget cuts imply reducing patient care quality, unless you "stretch" the truth to secure more funding. Think through these dilemmas carefully: what is the moral principle at stake. Where do you draw the line. How would you phrase your refusal or your alternative proposal. By rehearsing these responses in your head, you build mental reflexes. You reduce the risk of freezing or conceding when the real challenge surfaces.

Find allies who share your principles. It is easier to hold firm when you know you are not alone. Whether it is a colleague, a mentor, or a community of like-minded professionals, your support network can reinforce your stance. If you face an ethical dilemma about a project's safety standards, having a trusted co-worker who agrees with your concerns can bolster your confidence to speak up. You are not a lone voice in the wilderness. Even if you cannot find allies in your immediate setting, you might connect with a broader network online or through professional associations. Moral solidarity often transforms a potential sacrifice into a manageable stand.

Setting boundaries is equally crucial. State them openly when you sense a risk of conflict. For instance, if you join a new organisation, make it clear upfront: "I cannot endorse any data manipulation. If the numbers do not look good, I would rather solve the root problem than hide it." By announcing your limits early, you condition others to respect them. If they know your stance, they are less likely to push you into shady territory. And if they try, you can reference your earlier declaration, reminding them that you have not changed your position.

In high-pressure environments, stress can fog your judgment. Maintain healthy coping mechanisms: exercise, reflective writing, or even brief moments of solitude. These routines act like emotional reset buttons, allowing you to clear your mind and reconnect with your principles before making big calls. If you let stress accumulate unchecked, you become susceptible to rash decisions that undermine your values. Keep your mental and physical health in good shape so you have the stamina for ethical battles.

Remember, staying true to your values does not imply rigidity in all things. You must remain adaptable in tactics but unwavering in ethics. You might find alternative solutions that satisfy broader objectives without betraying your moral code. Sometimes, creativity can turn what appears to be a lose-lose scenario into an innovative compromise. The difference is that you never compromise on the core principle itself. You stay flexible on implementation, not on integrity.

Lastly, accept the reality that holding your ground can come with a price. You might lose short-term gains or find yourself bypassed by those who prefer faster, less scrupulous methods. However, leadership built on shaky values always collapses under the weight of scandal, mistrust, or personal shame. In contrast, a stand taken under severe pressure can define your legacy as a leader of principle. People recall those who refused to cut corners, even if it meant swimming against the current. This brand of moral courage often outlives any immediate sacrifice. By anchoring yourself in unshakeable convictions, you ensure that no wave of pressure can pull you away from who you truly are.

4. The Daily Rituals of Great Leaders

Although vision and moral clarity define your overarching course, daily habits shape your actual progress. Leaders who reach the top and stay there rarely rely on spur-of-the-moment bursts of energy. They craft routines that prime them for sustained excellence, day after day. These rituals vary between individuals but share a common aim: to steady the mind, sharpen focus, and ensure that vital tasks never slip through the cracks of a hectic schedule.

Begin with how you start each morning. The best leaders often rise early, setting aside quiet time before the world intrudes. Some might use this window to read, reflect, or map out the day's priorities. Others exercise to ignite their physical and mental energy. The key is not the specific activity but the intention behind it. By choosing how you spend the first hour, you seize control of your time rather than reacting to demands as soon as you open your eyes. This sense of command fuels your confidence for the challenges ahead.

Another critical ritual involves planning and review. Whether it is a short evening reflection or a structured weekly debrief, you need a system to check what went well, what obstacles arose, and how to pivot for improvement. Leaders who skip this step risk drifting into reactive patterns. By taking even 10 minutes at day's end to evaluate performance, you spot inefficiencies early, celebrate small victories, and align tomorrow's tasks with long-term objectives. Over time, these incremental corrections accumulate, guiding you steadily towards your goals rather than leaving you buffeted by circumstance.

Mindful breaks also matter. Amid high-pressure roles, it is tempting to grind non-stop. Yet elite performers know that strategic pauses sharpen their edge more effectively than pushing to the brink of burnout. A short walk to clear your head, a deliberate lunch break with no screens, or a few minutes of focused breathing can restore your mental reserves. This is not indulgence; it is strategic recovery. Think of these pockets of rest as micro-renewals that keep your decision-making crisp and your temperament balanced. Without them, you risk spiralling into fatigue, irritability, and sloppy choices.

Another ritual that many notable leaders practise is proactive communication. Instead of drowning under an ever-growing mound of emails or messages, they designate specific windows to address inbound communication. They handle critical queries promptly, delegate what is not essential, and schedule more complex topics for face-to-face discussions or dedicated calls. By structuring communication habits, they avoid the endless ping-pong of scattered messages. This approach lets them maintain clarity in their daily workflow and ensures that crucial issues receive timely, focused attention.

Physical health cannot be overlooked. Some leaders incorporate a strict fitness routine, jogging, swimming, or resistance training, because they know a robust body underpins peak cognitive function. Others rely on consistent meal planning to avoid the quick-fix junk that dulls concentration over time. Prioritising physical well-being is not vanity. It is a foundational pillar that supports consistent performance. When your energy is stable, your mood is positive, and you handle stress with greater resilience.

Rituals should also include feeding the mind. Regular reading, whether in your field or outside it, expands your perspective and can spark fresh ideas. Some leaders blend this habit into daily downtime, reading a few pages while commuting or tackling a chapter before bed. Alternatively, they might consume podcasts or audio lessons during workouts. The aim is to keep the mind open and engaged. A stagnant intellect grows complacent, and complacency is the enemy of forward momentum.

Finally, each day's rituals should align with your deeper values and aspirations. If you proclaim that family is paramount but never carve out genuine time for them, your daily routines undermine your stated priorities. If you claim that developing others is crucial yet never schedule mentoring sessions, you contradict yourself. Your daily habits form the proof of your leadership convictions. This alignment between word and deed fosters authenticity. It is easy to talk about priorities; it is far more challenging and meaningful to inscribe them into your daily schedule.

By cultivating purposeful routines, you gain the discipline to thrive under pressure. These rituals create a sturdy rhythm where essential tasks are handled methodically, creativity flourishes, and stress does not derail your focus. You transform from someone who reacts to someone who drives results, day in and day out. In short, daily rituals act as the invisible scaffolding that supports your ambition and keeps you advancing when others lose their grip. They might look mundane from the outside, but the compound effect of consistent good habits can catapult you beyond the reach of those who rely on occasional bursts of effort.

5. The Final Step: Walking the Path of Leadership Every Day

You have amassed the tools: a leadership philosophy that reflects your deepest principles, a code of honour that shields your integrity, a clear strategy for upholding values under pressure, and daily rituals that power your efficiency and resilience. Yet the true challenge begins now. Leadership is not a title you put on for official duties and then discard. It is a daily walk, a living practice that weaves itself into every facet of who you are at work, at home, and in the broader community.

This is the point where many falter. They gain the knowledge but fail to integrate it into consistent action. Perhaps they apply these ideas only within the confines of their job, ignoring them in personal relationships or moral decisions outside work. Real leadership calls you to live by your code everywhere, not just in boardrooms or professional settings. The person you are at your most private moments should reflect the same ethics and discipline that you display to your team. Otherwise, you cultivate a double life that eventually corrodes your credibility.

Begin by reminding yourself daily why you chose this path. Leadership carries weighty responsibility. It demands sacrifice, accountability, and occasional loneliness. If you forget your core reasons, whether it is to uplift your family, inspire your organisation, or serve a greater cause, you risk drifting into cynicism or burnout. Reflect on your motives during quiet moments, perhaps in the early morning or late evening. Let that sense of purpose reinvigorate you, ensuring you do not lose sight of the bigger picture when minor frustrations arise.

Next, practise self-awareness. Each day, notice how you handle interactions. Did you snap at a colleague because you were short on time. Did you skirt a moral boundary when faced with a temptation. Did you shy away from giving honest feedback for fear of confrontation. Pinpoint these moments and ask yourself how they align with your stated code. This awareness is the beginning of real change. If you find yourself repeatedly slipping in a specific area, say, controlling your temper, focus on targeted improvements there. Over time, you close the gap between your intentions and your actions, forging a more harmonious leadership style.

Another crucial element is adaptability. The world changes, and so do the people you lead. Methods that worked last year might lose relevance tomorrow. Your unshakeable core is your moral centre, but your tactics should evolve. Embrace new technologies, learn from fresh voices, and remain open to shifting trends. This does not mean drifting aimlessly; it means staying flexible and creative within the boundaries of your principles. Such fluidity shows that you are not rigidly stuck in old patterns but are willing to adapt for the good of the mission.

Do not underestimate the power of small acts. You might be tempted to think leadership only shows up in grand gestures or big decisions. In reality, every moment you listen with full attention, every time you refuse to join petty gossip or every instance you praise someone's progress, you reinforce the culture you want to build. Small, consistent choices accumulate into a reputation that people respect. They form the invisible backbone of your leadership persona.

Finally, accept that the journey does not end. Mastery in leadership is never fully complete. There is always another dimension to explore, a new crisis to handle, a novel technique to learn, another up-and-coming leader who needs your mentorship. This sense of continuous pursuit should inspire rather than intimidate you. It keeps complacency at bay and ensures you do not stagnate. Each day is a fresh chance to apply your code and refine your craft, turning leadership into a lifestyle rather than a transient role.

And so you stand at the threshold, equipped with all the insights and tools gleaned throughout this book. The rest is in your hands. Will you let these lessons become dormant notes, or will you transform them into lived realities. The choice belongs to you alone. By walking the path of leadership every day by holding yourself accountable to a higher standard, you embody the potential that once felt distant. Your example will draw others who yearn for authentic, principled guidance. In that unity lies the real triumph: a group of people bonded by mutual trust and shared vision, bringing tangible hope and progress to the world.

Conclusion

This is your moment of resolve. You have travelled through the foundations of self-leadership, tested yourself under pressure, learned the nuances of influence, and uncovered the paradoxes that give true leadership its depth. Now, with a defined leadership philosophy, a personal code of honour, and practical rituals that ground you each day, you possess everything you need to thrive. Yet all the knowledge in the world means little unless you choose to act on it consistently.

Remember, leadership is not a certificate you earn. It is a commitment you renew daily. As you step forward, your tasks may vary- running a company, leading a community project, raising a family, or guiding a sports team- but the same principles apply. You serve, you stand firm on core values, you adapt without betraying your moral centre, and you elevate those around you. When you inevitably face setbacks, lean on the code you have built. When your successes multiply, stay humble and remember why you began this journey in the first place.

The future awaits your contribution. By walking the path of leadership every day, you carry the promise of positive change. You become a steady hand in a world that often feels unsteady. You become a voice of integrity where many go silent. You become a beacon of resilience when challenges loom large. And, above all, you become the leader who inspires others to discover their own strength, forging a legacy that will echo long after you have passed on the torch. This is the climax of your leadership quest, and it is also your beginning. Embrace it fully, and may every step you take light the way for those who follow

Printed in Great Britain
by Amazon